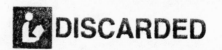

Beyond Top Secret U

Beyond Top Secret U

EWEN MONTAGU

PETER DAVIES : LONDON

Peter Davies Limited
15 Queen Street, Mayfair, London W1X 8BE

LONDON   MELBOURNE   TORONTO
JOHANNESBURG   AUCKLAND

Printed in Great Britain by
Willmer Brothers Limited, Birkenhead

Contents

Foreword

To many of our fellow-citizens, Mr Ewen Montagu is known as a distinguished judge, who sees to the heart of a matter, does not suffer fools too gladly, and has a certain sympathy with rogue characters. By those who were involved in the secret intelligence war against Germany he will always be remembered as Commander Montagu of N.I.D. 17M, the naval intelligence officer who was 'on the Ultra list', handling those 'most secret sources' for the Admiralty, and who, as a natural consequence, became its representative on 'the XX Committee'. This was the policy-making body in control of 'double-agents': the German spies whom we captured and 'turned round'. It was a marvellous piece of luck that the officer who handled naval 'Ultra' happened to be, in civil life, a barrister, trained to see the point of view, and anticipate the reactions, of an equally acute opposing counsel. Such training fitted him ideally for his second task; the task of defeating the German Secret Service, the Abwehr, at its own game and using it not to inform but to mislead, and sometimes vitally mislead, the German General Staff.

By chance, I happened to be a witness of the very beginning of this game. How little we then thought that it would grow into an engine of strategy! Even its original architect, Captain T. A. Robertson, whose genius guided the whole machine throughout the war, cannot have envisaged such triumphs. But who then could have guessed that we should possess the great boon of Ultra, and should be able to watch, day by day, the intimate

internal workings of our adversary? Who could have forecast
that every German spy in England would be working for us, and
would be believed by his German paymasters, and that we should
have, among those spies, such artists as 'Tricycle', 'Tate' and
'Garbo'? How well I remember those early beginnings: the first
wartime agents who came over in the dramatic summer of 1940
and the dimly perceived operations of 'Ast. Hamburg' which
were to lead us gradually into the heart of the Abwehr. It was
the earliest of these naval operations – the voyage of the good
ship *Theseus* and the furtive expedition to the Arctic island of Jan
Mayen – which brought Commander Montagu from Hull and
first brought me into touch with him. That was nearly two years
before the Abwehr 'Enigma' cipher was broken; but it showed
what might be done, and it was the beginning of a long associa-
tion.

The most spectacular single episode in the history of deception
was the now famous 'Operation Mincemeat' of 1943. Ewen
Montagu, more than any other man, was personally responsible
for that project, and has already written about it; but his book,
The Man Who Never Was, was published before the 'Ultra'
secret was out. So was Sir John Masterman's *The Double-Cross
System*, which had been written as an internal memorandum –
surely one of the most exciting internal memoranda in the history
of bureaucracy – in 1945. This book is not a repetition of either
of those works. It is Mr Montagu's own story of his war, of which
'Mincemeat' was only one incident, written freely, in the post-
Ultra era.

Having watched, from inside (as it seemed), both the German
and the British secret intelligence services at war, I have often
been tempted to make comparisons, and contrasts. One of the
contrasts was in the quality of the officers who actually did the
work. Of course the Germans did not have Ultra. But equally
they did not have imagination. We had many intelligence officers
who, in this respect, could compete with the Germans. But we
also had some who combined the traditional virtues of their
service with unconventional ideas, originality, flair. They also
had a sense of humour and entered – as did their best double

agents – with gusto into the unorthodox but serious game. I could name several such officers. One of the most enterprising and original was the author of this enjoyable and accurate book.

Chiefswood,   Hugh Trevor-Roper
Melrose.

Author's Note

Most people who served in the last war were taught that the highest classification of secrecy for documents was Top Secret, although Most Secret was the British equivalent classification until the United States entered the war. Only those directly concerned with the production and use of deciphered enemy messages, whether from the Enigma machine or from other sources, knew that there was a still higher classification Ultra Secret, designated by a stamp Top Secret U, which warned those in the know that the document had to be dealt with according to the relevant regulations but gave nothing away to the uninitiated.

But even the comparatively very few who were in the Ultra, the Top Secret U, picture did not necessarily know that there was yet another classification, sometimes overlapping but always beyond Top Secret U; this classification comprised any document disclosing 'double-cross' work, deception through double agents; these could not be shown to anyone other than the very few who were directly concerned with such work.

During the war I was fortunate enough to be concerned in this double-cross work as well as with Ultra but I never thought that I would be able to tell even my friends what I had been doing beyond the fact that I was in Naval Intelligence.

Then, in 1953, I quite suddenly had a wholly unexpected stroke of luck and *The Man Who Never Was*, a book describing a most unusual piece of deception in which I was involved, was published.

Duff Cooper wrote his delightful novel *Operation Heartbreak,* using as a basis the floating of a corpse to the coast of Spain with documents intended to deceive the Germans. This idea was based on just one of the deception operations that I had been engaged in, Operation Mincemeat, so the security authorities 'flapped', and that naturally leaked to Fleet Street. The leaks grew until able and energetic reporters were getting accounts of what had happened and, as these came from Germans, Spaniards and others who had to try to explain away their mistakes, the stories were largely fiction. The security authorities came to the conclusion that the form of Operation Mincemeat was so different from that of our other deception successes that no harm could come from its publication, whereas some of the untrue statements which would otherwise be published could be highly damaging.

So I was suddenly asked to write the true story and to get it published in time to kill the false ones, and *The Man Who Never Was* was written. It was done in one week-end, with a lot of black coffee and literally no sleep – something that any busy barrister is used to when preparing to 'open' a long and complicated case. My memory and some papers that I had been specially allowed to keep were my only 'brief and instructions'.

That book has had an astonishing success. Nearly two million copies were sold, it was published in fifteen languages and is still in print and selling after twenty-four years. There was also a film of the same name with a brilliant script by Nigel Balchin which is still shown from time to time on TV.

As a result of all this I have been pressed ever since, by friends and by publishers, to write some more. 'You must have had other thrilling experiences,' they would say. I had indeed, for Operation Mincemeat was just one incident in my work during some six months out of my six years service. At that time there were good security reasons why the rest should not be disclosed. Gradually, however, leaks grew and articles and books were written, although not of course by those who had been engaged in the work themselves, who all maintained an honourable silence in spite of the stroke of luck that had fallen to me.

As a result the powers-that-be gradually relaxed the ban. Sir

John Masterman was eventually allowed to publish his definitive book *The Double-Cross System* on how double agents were, and should be, run. Nevertheless, I could not tell the story of 'my war' without bringing in our achievements based on the breaking of German and other enemy ciphers – and I was persuaded that there were good reasons why that should not be done, in spite of partially accurate articles written by people who, though they were of great distinction, could not bring the authority of having been really in the work.

Now the situation has changed and some of the security restrictions have been relaxed. So I have attempted in this book to set down how I had the luck to be involved in interesting and exciting intelligence work.

I relate how I came, through double-cross work through double-agents, to take part in the strategic and other general deceptions, including those about V-bombs and D-Day, and became in practice the only source through which the German espionage service obtained regular British naval information. It is *not* a history or text book about double-cross work.

I relate how I also read, and worked with, all the messages that we intercepted and deciphered, and thus had the fascinating experience of studying simultaneously the thoughts and plans of our Chiefs of Staff and those of Hitler and his High Command, besides taking part in the battle against the German Military Intelligence Service. But it is *not* a history of Special Intelligence, Ultra Secret work, as it was called, for that would require access to all of the documents and would result in an entirely different type of book.

This book is written from a purely personal point of view, it is based on an excellent memory for events and conversation, together with some memoranda which, in very special circumstances and for a very particular reason, I was allowed to keep. These did not always record dates, so the sequence of events, as well as some minor details, may not always be accurate where that did not affect the development of my work at the time. I have also refreshed my memory on some points from Sir John Masterman's book.

There is another thing that I should mention here. Excellent though my memory has always proved to be, there has always been one dreadful gap in it. I have *never* been able to remember names, a failing which will not, I hope, offend those affected.

Finally, may I end this Note by stressing that all that was achieved was achieved by team-work. Nothing could have been done by one or two people alone, and we all brought something from our background and past experience into the common pool. In my case it was, perhaps, the experience of an advocate. An advocate, if he is to be any good, has to ask himself, before he says anything to a judge or jury, 'How will that argument or bit of evidence appeal to the hearer?' and *not* 'How does it appeal to me?' And, he has to ask himself, 'Is there another bit of evidence which would help our case?' Whenever I had posed that last question, I had to content myself with enquiring whether it existed. Now I could build on that experience and just invent the bit of evidence, something which I could never have done in my professional work, but which would be a crooked lawyer's dream of heaven!

But I cannot stress too strongly that the use that was made of Special Intelligence was the product of all the members of my Section of the Naval Intelligence Division, and the deception work was that of the Double-Cross Committee and Section B.1A* of M.I.5., to all of whom I am deeply grateful.

Ewen Montagu
Warren Beach
Beaulieu

* See glossary of terms, p. 179.

Prologue

It really all started the year before. Early in 1938 I had become convinced that another war was inevitable and, having been born in 1901, my recollections of 'The War to End Wars' had convinced me that there were better ways of dying than in a modern army. In any of the Services you could be shot or blown to bits, but in the Navy or R.A.F. one would live reasonably clean and would not die by drowning in mud, as so many of my near contemporaries had done.

The R.A.F. was 'out' as the whole world spins round as soon as my feet get four feet above ground level. Sailing had been my mania ever since I had started about five years before. Surely the Navy might find some use for me.

To my joy, the Admiralty formed the R.N.V.(S.)R. – the supplementary reserve. This was simply a list of people who had some knowledge of seamanship, boat handling and navigation, who were ready to be called up on the outbreak of war and who the Navy felt might, with training, make officers. There were no drills or periods of annual training, a factor of importance to me with a busy junior practice at the Bar.

So I applied to join and went to H.M.S. *President*, conveniently moored at the foot of Middle Temple Lane, for my 'medical'.

I was accepted, and all that the Admiralty asked of us at a subsequent lecture was that we should keep up our qualifications and, if possible, learn morse and semaphore.

After crewing in *Latifa* in the Fastnet race in August 1939, I raced my own boat, *John Dory*, from Plymouth to La Rochelle, winning the small class. Then we picked up my wife and sailed via La Baule and Belle Isle to Beg Meil where she had been 'bucket and spading' with the two children. There, for the first time for days, we listened to the radio news and heard that war was likely and that all Britons were advised to leave France.

What was to turn out to be my last sail for seven years was a heart-warming fast run up Channel, hard on the wind, in glorious weather and escorted for over an hour by porpoises playing round our bow – scraping into the Solent on the last of the tide just before midnight on the Friday–Saturday night before war was declared.

I was 'called up' to go with the first batch to H.M.S. *King Alfred*, the principal municipal swimming baths in course of construction at Hove, where R.N.V.R. officers were to be trained throughout the war. At that moment I ceased to be Ewen Montagu, K.C., and became 'Probationary Temporary-Acting-Sub-Lieutenant Montagu, R.N.V.R.' I couldn't but admire the cautious way in which the Admiralty kept its options open – three ways of getting rid of one! (As our Petty Officer instructors were to point out to us, 'the lowest known form of marine life'.)

This is not the book in which to relate my experiences in H.M. 'ships' *King Alfred* and *Beaver*, interesting though they were. But, because they had a great effect on my personal development as a naval officer and the way in which my war service developed, I should record just a few incidents.

From the very first day of operations in the *King Alfred* the staff of that 'ship' began, not only to train us in the skills which we would need, navigation, seamanship, gunnery and so on, but also to instil into us what was almost more important – the spirit of the Navy and discipline.

Our very first experience, after reporting back from our billets on the day after our arrival, was morning Divisions, our first parade. After the roll-call came the first order 'Fall out the Roman Catholics'. I thought that these would be marched off for separate prayers and that there would be a further order applying to others who were not Church of England, including Jews like myself. But not a bit of it. Next came the lovely Naval Prayer:

O Eternal Lord God, who alone spreadest out the heavens and rulest the raging of the sea; who hast compassed the waters with bounds until day and night come to an end; Be pleased to receive into thy Almighty and most gracious protection the persons of us thy servants, and the Fleet in which we serve. Preserve us from the dangers of the sea, and from the violence of the enemy; that we may be a safeguard unto our most gracious Sovereign Lord, King George, and his Dominions, and a security for such as pass on the seas on their lawful occasions; that the inhabitants of our Island may in peace and quietness serve thee our God; and that we may return in safety to enjoy the blessings of the land, with the fruits of our labours, and with a thankful remembrance of thy mercies to praise and glorify thy Holy Name; Through Jesus Christ our Lord.

Amen.

I am temperamentally allergic to what might be called 'group praying' in a set service, regarding prayers as essentially a direct and personal matter between the Almighty and oneself, but at that moment, with a group of us dedicating ourselves together to a common effort in anticipation of unknown dangers, saying *that* prayer together was exactly right and a most moving experience. To me that prayer, with which we started our war service, has always seemed to sum up the whole spirit, dedication and comradeship of the Navy. Although I was later told that the traditional order was to enable anyone, besides Roman Catholics, who wished to do so to fall out, I always 'stood fast' and took part.

When after some days, the staff decided gradually to tighten up discipline, there came another experience which affected me greatly. Commander Head, the Executive Officer, put a notice on the board which, roughly, read: 'The attention of all officers is drawn to K.R. and A.I. No. so-and-so which reads as follows';

and then quoted the passage in King's Regulations and Admiralty Instructions which prohibited officers from smoking a pipe on shore in uniform in public.

Many of us were pipe-smokers and we were on shore, in uniform and in public for most of our off-duty time. It seemed absurdly archaic and snobbish. To my joy I found in that morning's *Times* a photograph of Winston Churchill, with the usual cigar in his mouth, walking across Horse Guards' Parade with the First Sea Lord, Admiral Sir Dudley Pound, in uniform with gold from his wrist to his elbow – and a pipe in his mouth! I promptly cut the photo out (in spite of its being the Mess copy) and pinned it up on the board immediately below the other notice. Feeling rather clever I awaited the reaction.

Commander Head left both these on the board and pinned below them another notice which read:

Special arrangements have now been made whereby any officer at present under training in H.M.S. *King Alfred* may smoke a pipe on shore when in uniform and in public, in spite of K.R. and A.I. No. so-and-so ... when he becomes First Sea Lord.

I felt 'just so big'. Apart from that, there were thousands of wrong ways to handle the situation, but only one right one, and I realized that the Navy had unerringly picked that single right one. At that moment my admiration for, and devotion to, the Navy became fixed and has persisted to the present day, in spite of ups and downs.

Our training continued and we were posted off here and there as requirements for officers arose, most of us only partly trained. In my case, after one mis-posting, I had to go into the sick-bay with fairly acute ptomaine poisoning, and it was while I was there that my next posting came through. It was to the armed yacht *Alice*. She was 500 tons and was the motor yacht which Vanderbilt had chartered as tender to *Vim*, his America's Cup 12–metre, when racing over here, so she seemed likely to be a comfortable ship; besides that, a friend, Tom Martin, was also posted to her.

Disappointment followed. I had joined up to go to sea, to use my seamanship experience and to fight, and I had fondly thought that I had managed to avoid the danger of a shore job. However, as soon as I had left the sick bay and returned to duty I was called in to Commander Head who told me that my papers had arrived. Why, he demanded, had I concealed the fact that I was a K.C.? Lots of people could do Sub.'s jobs and 'you're not going to have a yachting holiday at the Government's expense – you're going to a proper job where your qualifications will count.'

Such argument as I could put up to a senior officer on such an occasion was of no avail and I was taken off normal training and given special reading to do. This was in any hut not in use during a particular period, and I mainly spent my time listening to the off-duty C.P.O. Instructors gossiping over cups of coffee. Thus I learnt more of how the Navy really works than I could have done in any other way, and acquired knowledge that stood me in good stead later on, as well as after the war when I became the Judge Advocate of the Fleet.

The result of all this was that I became the last remaining member of the first intake and, at a Guest Night, I was presented by the C.P.O. Instructors with 'The H.M.S. *King Alfred* Long Service and Good Conduct Medal' in a leg-pulling ceremony.

Then the blow that I had feared fell and I was posted to H.M.S. *Beaver*, the headquarters 'ship' of F.O.I.C. (the Flag Officer in Command) Humber, as Assistant S.O. (I) (Staff Officer, Intelligence). I left next day and reported to the H.Q. in Hull on 23 November 1939. I had been deprived of my wish to fight at sea but, all unknowingly, I was embarking on what I am sure was as fascinating a war as anyone could have hoped to have.

Apart from the intelligence work itself I was part of a very happy team in which we helped one another during the many bursts of activity, dealing with daily convoys, minesweeping (the minesweeping base was at Grimsby), the 5th Destroyer Flotilla (Lord Louis Mountbatten's famous and wonderfully efficient flotilla which was based at Immingham) and dealing with the fishing trawlers working out of Hull, Grimsby and Immingham as well as some of the minor ports.

Apart from 'flaps' and the enemy bombing and mining raids which soon started, the work was not very hard, though the hours were long.

At first the intelligence side was very dull but soon the S.O. (I), a Commander, was posted elsewhere and I was promoted to his job. From then on I was able to develop the intelligence work which, until then, had been chaotic. There was practically no liaison with any of the other Services or the police and, although the ships which arrived from Scandinavia had passed through German waters, and those from Holland had come from a country bordering on Germany and the Icelandic trawlers had much information about German activities there, and they and our own trawlers could tell much about the Luftwaffe's methods and activities in the North Sea, there was no systematic gathering of intelligence. The masters and skippers, tired from their voyages, were badgered haphazardly by all and sundry and consequently told little. I managed to get agreement by the other Services and the police that I should do any intelligence gathering necessary, after an approach geared to the characteristics of the particular seaman and his attitude to the war; I would then pass on the information obtained to all concerned.

This new system produced an ever-increasing volume of information which must have come to the notice of D.N.I. (the Director of Naval Intelligence) because, in November 1940, the Admiral sent for me to his 'cabin' and told me that D.N.I. had insisted, in spite of his protests, on my being posted to N.I.D. (the Naval Intelligence Division). I did not know whether to welcome this move or not. Apart from the fact that I was very happy in Hull where I was, to a considerable degree, 'running my own show', this would mean a definite end to any hope of my going to sea; on the other hand, if I was anyway to complete my war in intelligence, N.I.D. *was* the centre of things. But my feelings mattered little; I had been posted.

There was one further personal regret. I had been pressed, ever since the start of the war, by American friends to send my wife and children to the U.S., and Iris and I had given that question a lot of thought. Not only could we not be together, especially if I got to sea, but I had held various important positions in the Jewish community before the war, a fact well known to the Nazis, and a fact that would not be forgotten if they invaded Britain. Then Churchill made his speech about 'useless mouths' leaving the country on the same night as a fellow officer's children were killed by bombs unloaded on a farmhouse in the middle of the Yorkshire moors. So I persuaded Iris to go (naturally not knowing that I would soon be moved to London where we could get together) and on 17 July 1940, I said farewell to my family at Liverpool, wearing the uniform of a Lieutenant-Commander, to which rank I had just been promoted.

I

The Naval Intelligence Division*

N.I.D. was a very large Division of the Admiralty. It was also a
wonderfully efficient organization, the brilliant creation of one
man, Admiral J. H. Godfrey, C.B. (as he became). I have never
used the word genius of anyone else. I have been privileged to
know many extremely able and extremely wise men, at the Bar,
among Judges and among statesmen who came to my father's
house when I was a young man, but only to John Godfrey would
I give that accolade, certainly as regards intelligence work.

This tribute is the more sincere as, in most ways, I disliked
him as a person. It is only fair to say that this may largely be due
to a personality clash. As a barrister I had always been my own
master, running my own life and deciding myself how I did my
work. But it cannot have been that alone as not only did D.N.I.
very shortly after, allow me complete freedom of action in that
I had only to get authority for deception action where I felt that
I needed it, but my feelings were widely shared. It may well
have resulted from a deliberate policy by 'Uncle John', as he
was always known. The kindly image implied by the word
'Uncle' was completely false. His approach has been well summed
up in *Room 39*: 'Rear-Admiral John Godfrey was exacting,
inquisitive, energetic and at times a ruthless and impatient

* I should reiterate that this is *not* a history or text-book on the Naval Intelligence
Division. The definitive work in that respect can be found in Donald McLachlan's
Room 39 (Weidenfeld & Nicolson), although the security rules of the time when he
wrote necessitated his dealing only broadly and scantily with the work of the
Operational Intelligence Centre (O.I.C.) and of my section (17M).

master.' Someone else who knew him well has said that his method was to *drive* everyone to the limit – and, one might almost say, beyond. It is only fair to admit that it worked. We admired his genius so much that we 'took it' from him, and in his time as D.N.I. no one ever 'came off his toes'. Ye Gods, how we worked!

The Director of Naval Intelligence at the Admiralty was in a unique position. The invaluable and omniscient mystique of Admiral 'Blinker' Hall's powerful regime in the first war still endured. D.N.I. reported direct to the First Sea Lord and to the First Lord and, as John Godfrey developed his power, signals for 'D.N.I. only' were only sent to him – with no other circulation, whatever their subject. John Godfrey was hand-picked for the post and he had the inestimable advantage of being appointed in January 1939 as war was seen to be inevitable, so that he had the opportunity to make preparations, and select subordinates, from both within the Navy and from civilian life, in good time.

Among those who should be mentioned at this stage were his two invaluable trouble-shooters and, one might really say 'wanglers' – Ian Fleming and Ted Merrett. The former was a Lieutenant-Commander then Commander R.N.V.R. (Special Branch) and the latter remained a civilian, and they were designated as D.N.I.'s Personal Assistants, with no routine responsibilities.

Uncle John's room was in Room 38 off which there opened the office of his personal staff in Room 39. There his own Section, Section 17, was also located. Just along the corridor one way was the Deputy Director's room; then that of A.D.N.I., the Assistant Director, who was traditionally a Royal Marine officer and was responsible for security. Spread around there were the basic Sections, the Country Sections, Home, German, French, Scandinavian, etc., all numbered. There were also outside Sections at places like Oxford and Cambridge. For instance the Topographical Section which was nominally inter-Service, but was Uncle John's child: it produced what might be termed illustrated guide books for any countries that we might raid or invade. (It was of course Uncle John who had the brilliant idea of a public appeal for holiday snaps of beaches. It was, indeed, a photo of grannie having a picnic tea against a breakwater which gave the *only* basis from which could be calculated the slope of the Dieppe beach which invading tanks would have to climb.)

But most important of all was the Operational Intelligence Centre (the O.I.C.) which dealt with naval operational intelligence – mainly deciphered German naval signals – without which the U-boat war could not have been won.

That, then, was broadly the set-up of the organization, but one or two other big factors should be mentioned here. John Godfrey was not only a brilliant navigator and ship-handler (his last appointment before he became D.N.I. had been as Captain of the battle-cruiser H.M.S. *Repulse*) but he had lectured at the Royal Naval College at Greenwich and had studied the intelligence work of 'Blinker' Hall and the other combatants in World War I. He understood that frequently operational commanders could not make full use of intelligence because they could not assess its reliability – all, or virtually all, items of intelligence being passed on as 'from a usually reliable source'.

Uncle John devised the scheme that the Intelligence officer should *always* grade the intelligence and pass it on with that grading. Each source was graded from the Intelligence officer's experience of it on a scale from A to E; the accuracy of the particular item from 1 to 5. (A.1 was virtually reserved in practice for deciphered signals, etc.) Thus one might have B.3 to mean a very reliable source, who N.I.D. believe from other information may have got a very doubtful bit of information, or even B.5 – a very reliable source considered by N.I.D. to have, on this occasion, picked up gossip or made a mistake. On the other hand D (a very unreliable source) could get a D.1 or a D.2 by picking up a piece of information that other facts available to N.I.D. led them to judge as almost certainly accurate.

N.I.D. was not allowed to pass on anything without grading it, and this not only made *us* think but it was of the utmost help to the recipient who could not have the background knowledge that we had.

Moreover, John Godfrey also succeeded in persuading his fellow Directors, and the Secret Intelligence Service (S.I.S. or M.I.6) to use this system – and they had to be kept up to it. I remember, in the few weeks that I was in the Home Section, getting a piece of ungraded information from the War Office. It was one that I had to show to Uncle John and he immediately told me to make a copy and use it (so as not to waste time) but to let him have the original back. I learnt that he had returned the original to D.M.I. with a note asking what use this information was as it was ungraded. The result of notes of this kind was that the other Services did, eventually, always grade. At the same time such notes (which were typical) did not endear D.N.I. to his colleagues – and the result, as we shall see, was that the first time that he made a slip, several knives went into his back.

One could almost say that if John Godfrey had done nothing more during the war than institute this system, he would have deserved well of his country – as I could well understand when I began to read (as will be seen) the messages that the Germans got from *their* intelligence service. But there was so much more.

Those who both knew John Godfrey and had known 'Blinker' Hall were convinced that even that famous former Director could not have coped with the complexities that his successor faced, nor have devised and set-up the organization (both naval and inter-Service) to deal with them. Just to instance two: the O.I.C. to get the speed of action needed in a war which (apart from anything else) included aircraft; and the Joint Intelligence Committee consisting of the three Service Directors, 'C' (the Head of the Secret Intelligence Service) and a few others to co-ordinate intelligence work. He also sensibly got a chairman from the Foreign Office so as to avoid inter-Service jealousy.

Finally I must record two inflexible rules that Uncle John laid down for N.I.D. Items of intelligence must always be passed on 'un-edited'. Any views that we might have about the source, the message, or its content must always be separated from the item itself by the word 'Comment'. Secondly, we must never try to influence action by suppressing information or by weighting the number or type of message promulgated. Influence could only be exerted by separate notes or memoranda.

This then, broadly, was the organization that I joined on 16 November 1940.

2

The Home Section

Having reported to Room 39 I was taken in to Uncle John. We had a short chat during which he told me that he had noticed the way that intelligence gathering had been re-organized in the Humber and the quality and quantity of information that we had been passing to N.I.D. He then told me to report to the Home Section where I would be working 'for the time being', dealing particularly with Ireland and Iceland.

After the information that we had got at Hull I knew a good deal about what was going on in Iceland. But why Ireland? I never learned the answer. It became obvious that the real reason for my going to that Section at all was so that Uncle John could have a personal close-up of me, before letting me into the Ultra-Secret super-secret picture. Iceland alone was obviously not enough to keep me occupied. It might just be worth recording, to show how Churchill, with all the cares of running the war, never missed a detail however small, that it was he who issued one of his famous quarter-page directives that those two countries were always to be referred to as Ireland (R) and Iceland (C) to avoid confusion through mis-hearings, typist's errors or bad handwriting.

My colleagues in the Section were not only able but delightful people to work with. Several had a good sense of humour and they had accumulated a collection of 'garbled' signals which they pinned on the wall of our large room.

The Head of the Section was a very able and efficient active-service officer who was shortly to go back to sea as soon as he was fit again. Once he submitted to the then D.D.N.I. for approval a memorandum to go to 'All S.O.(I).s'. That D.D.N.I. had won a prize for 'English' while at Dartmouth, and had never been able to forget it. The memo was returned marked 'Approved – but surely it should be "All S.O.s (I)" '. The Head of the Section (after action) returned it to D.D.N.I. with 'Noted – but submitted that S.O.(I).s is hallowed by tradition. Surely no one speaks or writes of all M.s.P.' There was no reply.

Later the memory of that prize at Dartmouth was to intrude again. Charles Morgan, the writer, had been to Osborne or Dartmouth but had soon found himself to be a misfit and had left the Navy. Now Uncle John had brought him back to edit a pocket magazine which was circulated to all ships and establishments to bring news of what the Navy was doing and thinking. Before publication the material had to be passed by D.D.N.I. I happened to be speaking to D.D.N.I. in his room when the door was flung open, Charles Morgan came in clutching corrected proofs. He was white and shaking with rage. He said in an icy tone, 'I never rose higher in the Navy than a "snotty" and you can correct anything that I say about the Navy – but I'm regarded as the greatest living master of English and you are NOT going to correct my grammar.' And he slammed out of the room 'taking the door handle with him', as the expression goes.

Meanwhile I had taken up quarters at my mother's house in Kensington. It was a big one, with four floors and a large basement in Kensington Court. Besides mother, I found there my sister (who was working at W.V.S. Headquarters) and her husband-to-be; Mabel, who had been 'in the family' for more than thirty-five years already, as well as Nancy, one of the best cooks in London who had been one of us for nearly as long, while Ward, the butler, who had become a war-service policeman, was there in his off-duty hours. Our little community was completed by an ever-growing number of people, from a variety of sources and backgrounds, who had been 'bombed out', together with the wife of a Belgian officer serving with our Army.

It was an amusing community. All were busy by day, even

mother who was well over sixty; her hobby, and her genius all her life, had been 'entertaining', and she had a vast number of foreign friends; her contribution was to run a haven, not only for all those whom I have mentioned who came to live in the house, but also for a steady flow of overseas visitors – many of whom assisted in making this possible by sending food parcels which helped to provide for their successors. All of us who lived in the house slept on camp-beds in the basement rooms, making sorties to deal with fire bombs on our roof or in the streets.

Public transport from Kensington to the Admiralty has always been virtually impossible and petrol was too precious. So I dug out an old bicycle and learned how mountainous London really is. The exercise was good for me, especially as my job in the Home Section was very undemanding, even with occasional night duty – a most welcome relaxation after the strenuous life at Hull. In fact I had enough time available for Uncle John to put me on to a special job.

It had occurred to that ingenious mind that Hitler was believed to have an immense faith in his pet astrologer. What, thought Uncle John, if one could know what periods Hitler would consider to be his lucky ones. It *might* help, as it *might* indicate when Hitler was most likely to 'start something' or take a risk. But a difficulty was that you could be sure that all astrologers seemed to work on different calculations, and any six, given the same factors, could be relied on to give six different horoscopes. Then, he thought, one *might* get round that if one tried a lot of astrologers and if experience showed, as time went on, that the lucky periods in one horoscope did in fact coincide with times when Hitler took a plunge, one would at least have something to work on.

So Ted Merrett and I were sent round to a vast number of astrologers. The results were very entertaining but useless. However, it *might* have worked and, surely, was well worth trying.

Soon my initiation in the Home Section ended. Apparently I had passed close-up scrutiny (of which I was, in fact, unaware) and D.N.I. appointed me to what I believe to have been the most fascinating job of the war, a job in which I knew in advance practically every secret of the war, including the atom bomb, read the deciphered messages from enemy and neutral sources, and became part of the *German* spy-system in this country – indeed its only regular and 'reliable' source of naval intelligence!

3

Special Intelligence - Ultra

When John Godfrey took over as Director of Naval Intelligence he found in N.I.D. a small Operational Intelligence Centre (O.I.C.), which had been established by his predecessor to process, plot and then promulgate to the Fleet intelligence of immediate operational urgency. This, it was originally thought, would be based mainly on High Frequency Direction Finding (HF/DF – always known picturesquely as Huff Duff).

But Uncle John was determined that the operational authorities should not be let down. He envisaged the possibility that deciphered signals might develop into something of far greater operational importance than it was in the First World War, and of tactical as well as of strategic importance. Once again it was that unique 'intelligence instinct' of his which, before anyone else, recognized that such intelligence might play an almost decisive role in the war.

So the O.I.C. (numbered Section 8) grew under the guidance first of Paymaster-Commander (Ned) Denning (as the future Admiral Sir Norman Denning then was) and later of both him and retired Admiral Clayton (serving in the rank of Captain). It had a number of sub-sections, probably the most important of which was Section 8s. This started as the U-boat plotting section, the moving spirit of which was Rodger Winn (the future Lord Justice Winn); he was then a civilian and later, when he had taken charge of the sub-section, Captain R.N.V.R. (Special Branch) – the Special Branch being composed of untrained civilians who were given naval rank; they were given such rank as their superiors thought to be justified by their jobs outside the normal Navy rules of promotion.

John Godfrey realized that in this war, unlike the last, things would be too big for a naval cipher-breaking unit such as 'Blinker' Hall had run. Now it would have to be run on an inter-service basis and he acceded to the pressure of Sir Stewart Menzies ('C', the Head of M.I.6, the Secret Intelligence Service, which service was also known, confusingly enough, by his initial), pressure that the whole work of deciphering should be put under the control of M.I.6. Wireless signals, having been intercepted at various special receiving stations, were sent by teleprinter to Bletchley Park (B.P.) where they were deciphered and distributed. The product was known as 'Special Intelligence' and deciphered messages or documents about the subject were marked Most Secret – U.*

It is interesting that even today it is still sometimes claimed that John Godfrey was unwilling to co-operate with the other Services, whereas contemporary documents (and the memory of those really in the top-level picture) show that his was the foresight leading to the establishment of most of the inter-service intelligence co-operation. Originally this misapprehension may have stemmed from John Godfrey's unfortunate methods of driving rather than leading.

I have to stress this here because in his *The Ultra Secret*†, Group-Captain Winterbotham complains that the unco-operativeness of Admiral Godfrey was the cause of the Admiralty insisting on handling Special Intelligence differently from the other Services. That error may not be the fault of the author, who may not have been as familiar with the way in which the war was conducted at the highest level as he thought, invaluable though the part was that he played in safeguarding the cryptographer's

---

* Later, after the Americans had pointed out that to them the word 'most' could mean 'almost', we altered this to Top Secret—or, in regard to Special Intelligence Top Secret U – the U being for Ultra. Anything so marked was only circulated to named persons on a very restricted list – otherwise the information in the deciphered signal or document had to be paraphrased and its provenance most carefully camouflaged.

† *The Ultra Secret* by Group-Captain Winterbotham (Weidenfeld & Nicolson).

work in the deciphering of the most important part of Special Intelligence. He clearly has not realized that the Admiralty, unlike the War Office and the Air Ministry, which were administrative bodies, was an active operational command and had to have *all* intelligence in one spot, without any delay. Even the highest grade signals and telegrams which were sent out in a machine cipher, were not the whole of intelligence, not even the whole of Special Intelligence.

Let us assume, for example, that a German battleship is being chased round the Atlantic and that the pursuing ships have temporarily lost contact. In those circumstances several authorities will be trying to solve the problem of where the German ship is heading. The senior Admiral on the spot will be in control of the pursuit. The Admiralty will not only have to keep the C-in-C informed of *all* available intelligence, from *all* sources, but also of any other ships which might be made available to help. The Admiralty will also have an independent over-all control, not only of the existing pursuit but also of the ordering of those additional ships to change their allotted tasks and assist in the operation, and of directing them into the right positions to support the C-in-C and to cut off the most likely routes of escape. It is only in the O.I.C., with its comprehensive world-wide picture, that there is both the knowledge of where those additional ships are and also the fullest Ultra-Secret information and the *experience with which to interpret it*. For instance a signal from Bordeaux might indicate that U-boats are being warned that a German ship is approaching a certain area; it might not say so specifically, but experience and Rodger Winn's flair will show that that is the right interpretation of a signal that says something quite different. Or, if a U-boat is ordered to try to protect the battleship's passage, only Winn and his Section 8s will know from what position the U-boat is likely to be moving – and even, sometimes, how many torpedoes she has left.

I give these examples because it is important that the reader should appreciate the reasons for, as well as the background to, the Admiralty set-up so as to understand the way in which the Special Intelligence part of my job developed. And I should stress again that the Enigma machine cipher (of which I will be

B

writing more later) was not the only German cipher of real value or of high level as Group-Captain Winterbotham's book tends to suggest. There was other Special Intelligence of all levels which was both invaluable in itself and also often threw a fresh light on the machine cipher messages. Indeed the way of dealing with the non-operational Special Intelligence, both machine and other ciphers, that John Godfrey devised and established was so much better than that of the other Ministries that, as will be seen, the Air Ministry eventually sent an officer to be trained to establish a Section like the one of which I was put in charge.

Non-operational Special Intelligence originated in this way. For some time early in the war, signals in a particular cipher were intercepted and broken (deciphered). They were few and of no naval interest. Then, in February 1940, came what were known as the Theseus messages which contained weather and shipping reports in the Norwegian coastal area as well as messages from German agents in that country. At first these were thought to come from a shore station, but it was eventually found that they in fact came from the German ship *Theseus* which, disguised as the Swedish ship, *Hese,* sailed up and down the Norwegian coast, sending her own reports and also transmitting reports picked up from agents in the ports at which she called. The checking of these signals started the co-operation between 'C' and N.I.D. on such messages. Consideration was given to trying to capture the ship but, owing to her cruising almost entirely in territorial waters, it was decided to do nothing about her.

Then, in the summer of 1940, Bletchley Park got, and the decipherers there broke, messages in the same cipher showing that the Germans were going to establish weather-reporting stations on Jan Mayen Island in the Arctic – a project which, as the messages showed, Goering considered to be of great importance to the German Air Force.

As the German expeditions were being prepared we kept in touch with all that was going on. When the stations had been established, we went there and duly 'collected' the personnel. As we knew exactly where they were it was easy, though other places had to be visited also in order to protect the source of our knowledge.

The Germans were much concerned at the silence of the stations and, after air reconnaissances, sent another expedition in October 1940. As a cruiser happened to be in the area she was directed into a position where she 'happened' to intercept the German ship concerned – which stranded herself and the personnel were captured. The Germans then gave up the Jan Mayen project which they had regarded as so important.

The N.I.D. end of this was all managed by two civilians in Section 17, D.N.I.'s personal section. It was, however, apparent that these messages were increasing in volume and naval interest. D.N.I. decided that someone would have to deal with this traffic and other non-operational Special Intelligence as a separate job. That was the first reason why I had been sent for from Hull.

4

Double Agents

A word now about double agents. Our double agents were people whom the Germans believed to be working for them, but whose movements, reports, etc., were controlled by us, so that we could decide exactly what information the Germans received through them. The great majority of double agents whom we used during the war fell broadly into three categories. First, those who volunteered to act in this way when they had been approached by the Germans in a neutral country. Secondly and more frequently, those who volunteered on arrival here. Then, most frequently of all, those who were captured on their arrival and then agreed to work for us. In the last category there were a number who so readily co-operated that they might have volunteered had we not picked them up before they could do so. There were also a fair number who came into our fold in other ways. Besides all these, there were a great number who did not really exist at all in real life, but were imaginary people notionally recruited as sub-agents by double agents whom we were already working.

From early in the war the Germans got no regular reports from this country except those which we supplied. Moreover, the Germans believed, and based their actions and planning on these reports. The only other information that they got, apart from occasional (usually low grade) reports from neutral seamen, was from occasional neutral visitors, and more regular reports from neutral diplomats. By 1943 we had established so much confidence in the double agents in the mind of the Germans that, where their reports differed from the reports that they got from these neutrals, our agents were always believed. This was confirmed at the time by what we read in Special Intelligence and it has been further confirmed by documents captured after the war, and other checks.

The purposes of running double agents are many and it may help if I list the major ones which, it will be seen, fall into two categories, which in themselves overlap : the enhancement of security for our side and the deception of the enemy. First, we controlled at least part – eventually all – the enemy espionage system in this country. A spy is difficult to infiltrate and still more difficult to maintain and, if we were giving the Germans a satisfactory service of information through their spies, they would not try to send many others. Even if they needed more spies, we could provide them as sub-agents.

Secondly, we gained knowledge of their methods and the stories which their spies were to use if caught. This supplemented what we learnt from Special Intelligence and made it easier to pick up any new spies that they did send. Sometimes the Germans had to provide extra funds for our double agents and we were able to pinpoint neutral diplomats who were ready to do this service for them. And we learnt details of their wireless procedures and ciphers which helped our interceptors and decipherers, as well as those who would have to interrogate later arrivals.

Thirdly, we got evidence of enemy intentions from the questionnaires that they brought and the questions sent to them. To give an obvious example: you don't tell an agent to report on beaches and communications and so on in South-West England if you intend to invade (or bomb) South-East England. And it may not be without interest if no instructions to any of the agents ask for information west of, say, Dungeness. The cessation of interest in a particular category of information may indicate abandonment of a plan. To repeat the example, if they tell their agents not to risk trying to report troop movements in the potential invasion area, it is some indication that invasion is abandoned, at least for the time being.

Fourthly, one can hope to influence German operations. For example, at one stage, on Air Ministry instructions, we got them to change bombing targets by exaggerating some anti-aircraft defences (which were weak) and playing down others (which were strong).

Fifthly, we learned much about the German weapon research and improvements from their questions about ours. And we were able to deceive them about our research and developments and our new weapons.

Sixthly, we could put over a lot of what we called 'ad hoc' deceptions, deceptions to gain either a short-term tactical advantage or a breathing space while some new weapon was being produced or an existing one improved.

Seventhly, and most important of all, we could try to gain the immense strategic advantage of deceiving the enemy about the place and time of our invasion of Europe. This was, of course, our major objective and our double agents played a crucial part in achieving this.

These are but some of the advantages to be gained. There were many others, including the deception to diminish the damage by bombing by V–1s and V–2s. But for all this one had to pay a price, small though that price was. If the Germans were to believe in, and rely on, our agents we would have to 'build them up'. They had to pass accurate information which the Germans would find confirmed by later events – and the higher the level of that information the better. One example was an accurate report sent by wireless that H.M.S. so-and-so (a major ship) was sailing tomorrow for Gibraltar. This could be done if we knew that no U-boat could be moved to intercept in time, or if the British ship's actual route was one that the Germans would not foresee. When her arrival at Gibraltar was duly reported to the Germans by their many spies among the Spanish workers there, it was a plus for the agent who had sent the report. Also, if an agent was instructed by the Germans to go to, say, Bristol he would have to report what he saw on the airfields visible from the railway. One Director of Intelligence (Air) vetoed an agent seeing and reporting fighter aircraft on one of those airfields until it was pointed out to him that a neutral diplomat, known to be in touch with the Germans, had made the same journey the day before! But it needed skill by the case-officers, the controllers of the agents, to ensure that we did not have to pay too much in order to keep the agents credible and to enhance their reputations.

Indeed great care was *always* taken to make sure that no true information of any movement or operation could ever reach the Germans in time for them to be able to use it to our detriment. It is important to stress this. Recently various writers who had no personal part in, or knowledge of, deception operations have spread a complete canard that the R.A.F.'s terrible losses in a raid on Nuremberg were due to the 'fact' that the Germans had been forewarned of the raid in order to increase the credibility of a double agent before he was used in the all-important deception to protect Operation Overlord, the landing in Normandy. This completely untrue story, which was then picked up by sensation-seeking journalists, must have caused great distress to the relatives of the gallant airmen who lost their lives in that raid. Such a wanton action (apart from being wholly unnecessary) would never have been given a moment's consideration by the Double-Cross Committee, and the story is completely untrue.

Finally, when one wanted to put over misinformation, one had to consider which agent could plausibly obtain it. Then, whether there was a real risk of the Germans learning (before D-Day) that it was untrue. Then, if there was such a risk, whether it could be put over in such a way that the Germans would consider it to be a mere mistake, for instance, a really good agent saying 'I've heard from someone I think is very reliable, but can't guarantee', if that would be effective enough to put the deception over. And whether, in a deception of some real importance, it was worth sacrificing an agent by letting him be 'blown' by the false information and whether one could do that without causing the Germans to get suspicious about other agents.

Before I became connected with double-cross work, M.I.5 had been running a double agent, code-name Snow – indeed both M.I.5 and M.I.6 had been operating him to some extent since the Germans had sent him over in pre-war days – and after the outbreak of war he and another double agent called Biscuit started being asked questions about our aircraft. M.I.5 applied to Air Commodore Boyle, then D. of I. Air, who vetted what might be transmitted by them. Indeed he had the courage to vet the answers to some innocuous naval and military questions.

Later M.I.5 allowed both Snow and Biscuit to meet their spy-master (the German Secret Service officer who controlled them), Major Ritter in Amsterdam, on more than one occasion. Something might have been deduced from the fact that Major Ritter suddenly informed them in April 1940 that another meeting was urgent but that Amsterdam would no longer be safe. He en-quired whether they could get to sea and rendezvous with a U-boat and, after consideration and consultation by M.I.5 with D.N.I., Snow replied that they could get passage in a trawler (the crew of which were anti-war) and rendezvous in the North Sea. Owing to weather conditions this rendezvous failed although both sides made efforts to achieve it.

By the summer of 1940 it was clear that an efficient system of providing approved information for transmission to Germany was needed. The Germans were sending over more and more agents and asking more and more questions – and with the dan-ger of invasion the vetting of what could be transmitted to Ger-many became more and more complex and difficult.

So the Directors of Intelligence set up an informal committee, which they called the W-Board, consisting of themselves, and a very few others, including the Intelligence Officer of the Com-mander-in-Chief Home Forces. At D.N.I.'s insistence they avoided giving themselves a 'charter' or 'directive', and the informal nature of the Board permitted really speedy work, with decisions given by the Director concerned, if necessary after con-sultation with one or more of the others.

Each Director informed his respective Chief of Staff that they 'had a means of getting misinformation to the enemy' and that this would necessitate passing some true information which would be kept 'innocuous'. They managed to convince their masters that the less the latter knew about such cloak and dagger activity the better. To the credit of the Chiefs of Staff, they accepted this, which resulted in both flexibility and speed of action.

Such speed was, of course, essential. When an agent was asked a question or given an order by the Germans, he might delay compliance for a little while, for instance so as to get leave of absence from his notional cover-job, or so as to wait for his 'day-off' in order that he could go and get the information, but sometimes an immediate answer was absolutely necessary. He obviously could not reply: 'I am waiting for permission to answer from the officer who supervises me, he has to get it from the controlling committee, they have to get it from their superiors and they in turn must get permission from the Chiefs of Staff – and the Chiefs of Staff are busy at the moment with much more important matters such as running the war.'

This problem was solved in a surprisingly commonsense way. Almost immediately, before the end of September, the volume of work was getting too much for reference to men with such enormous responsibilities as the members of the W-Board, in their turn, had to cope with. It was the Director of Military Intelligence who put up a proposal on September 26 that the W-Board should content themselves with supervising a working committee who would do the actual work, and suggested the name W-Section, later changed to the more apt Twenty (or double X) Committee.

The W-Board soon gave *carte-blanche* to the working section and, in my case, Uncle John soon gave me equal trust – relying on us to consult where we thought it necessary. Even the original broad mandate, which had been proposed by the then Director of Military Intelligence, that the working section's job was 'the collection, handling and dissemination of false information', was soon forgotten. We spent far more time collecting and passing true information to build up the credibility of agents in German eyes – and the benefits that we could disseminate in the way of true intelligence to *our own side* were very wide in their scope.

This, then, was the organization which was established so as to provide the information to be passed by the double-agents to the Germans – not only the false information with which to deceive the enemy but also the answers to questions and instructions given to those double agents by the German spy-masters who operated them – as well as a mass of other information. For, as I have indicated, in order to remain plausible in the eyes of his German masters, an agent in the United Kingdom would be expected to keep his eyes and ears open – to see, to listen, and to report.

For this reason each agent, according to his notional location, job and character, would have to send back to his masters a lot of information about what he would have seen and heard if he had been living the life that they supposed he was living. Lower grade agents would generally only be able to pick up small details or rumours, though these might well be important as corroboration of another, better, agent's reports – but he *might* see something of real significance on which the Germans might place great reliance if he had established himself in their eyes as being an accurate and observant reporter.

Similarly, in order to convince the Germans of the value and reliability of the higher grade agents, we *had* to provide these with a continuing flow of really important accurate, or at least undetectably false, information.

But all that provision and vetting of intelligence was only one facet of the work to be done – the part with which I was personally concerned. In addition someone had to look after the agents as they arrived and then, even more important, to decide and control all the background content of their messages. For this purpose M.I.5 had set up a special section, Section B.1 A, of most able officers, drawn from many walks of life, led by Lieutenant-Colonel T. A. R. (Tar) Robertson.

When a German agent arrives here he is a 'person' with a background and a character which together influence the type of job which the Germans can expect him to get over here, and the friends that they can expect him to make. So, whether he is in fact in custody or not, he has to be given a notional job, a notional home, notional friends and so on – all consistent with his personality. All this dictates what he can plausibly learn and report, just as his personality dictates the manner in which he acts and reports, acting courageously or cautiously, accepting and transmitting rumours or only reporting what he has real evidence about, sending only terse messages or 'writing them up'.

If he recruits sub-agents these may well be completely fictitious (notional is again the term that we used) but, nevertheless, each one would be built up through his messages as a real person and must *never* be allowed to step out of character.

And all of them, agents and notional sub-agents alike, had to suffer all the normal human vicissitudes (notionally, of course, in truth, but factually according to what the Germans had to be made to believe). More than fifty men and women could not go through some five years of war without getting ill, having to go through a period of overtime in their notional jobs so that they would have to miss some routine task (such as observation of the docks), losing a job and having to move their homes unwillingly, and so on – all matters which would cause a break in their messages or even change the whole pattern of what they could see and report. And, by the law of averages, some would be bound to be caught, or at least lose their nerve, or would decide to throw up their spying because the Germans could not manage to get their pay through to them – therefore ceasing transmission of reports either suddenly (as if they had been arrested) or after warning the Germans of what they were going to do.

All this required immense ability and careful documentation by the case officers, as the officers of Section B.1A allotted to the various double agents were called. I must stress how difficult it was to remember the characteristics and life pattern of each one of a mass of completely non-existent notional sub-agents, let alone his or her personal circumstances and 'quirks'. Any mistake could have 'blown' the credibility of that sub-agent and with him certainly the main agent – and, perhaps, even the whole double-cross operation. The responsibilities and difficulties of Section B.1A were indeed immense, and the way in which they coped was astonishing.

I will recount how four quite different agents, all of the highest grade, could be used together to put over a fairly typical deception, two giving different aspects of the main point and the other two 'just happening to pick up' seemingly unimportant facts which, at the receiving end, would be taken as corroborating and confirming that report. This sort of method was used quite frequently to put over deceptions other than the unimportant ones.

In late November 1942 the Admiralty decided that it would be a good thing if the Germans could be persuaded to keep, or even to increase, the existing number of U-boats in the Mediterranean where we, at the time, were able to cope with them quite well, and thereby reduce the number operating in the Atlantic, where our available escorts were far too few in that vast expanse of ocean.

The first agent, Balloon, who moved in what might be described as good circles, reported a conversation between a senior naval and senior army officer that he had overheard in his club to the effect that the Navy was very satisfied with the way the anti-U-boat war was going in the Mediterranean; we had concentrated all possible escort vessels, aircraft and technical apparatus and thought that there were signs of the U-boat giving up in despair. This would enable the Navy to transfer the main effort to the Atlantic where ... There then followed a good passage about the convoy losses in the Atlantic which necessitated a change of policy.

About a week later, Tate, one of our star agents, gave news from his girlfriend. She was completely fictitious and was notionally in a confidential position at the U.S. Naval Headquarters in Grosvenor Square and was often very indiscreet. She had notionally grumbled to Tate that she had had an awfully overworked few days as there had been a dispute between the British and American Naval Staffs. The British wanted to reorganize the convoy escorts and other protection of the routes in the North Atlantic owing to the losses there. The Americans were afraid that this would cause losses through the lowering of escorts and protection to the troops and supplies being taken to North Africa through the Mediterranean. The British had argued that the U-boat effort in the Mediterranean was under control. The British had won the arguments and ships and aircraft were being brought back from the Mediterranean.

Then Tricycle* joined in. He was another of our star double agents, a courageous and lively Yugoslav called Dusko Popov, who, while working hard, lived the life of a 'playboy' and was on personally friendly terms with some of his German spy-masters who managed him from Lisbon. This time we used him merely

* See *Spy-Counter-Spy* by Dusko Popov (Weidenfeld).

for a gossipy back-up story. He reported that he was in luck, as a friend, the captain of a corvette, was just back from the Mediterranean and was going to bring him back some nylon stockings from his next run to New York – these were unobtainable in London and nothing could please (or tempt) girls more!

Another double agent, Garbo, had a large team of completely notional sub-agents of varying grades spread around the United Kingdom. One of these reported that three destroyers had come into Milford Haven; he had overheard some of their officers grousing in a cafe; they were fed up as they had hoped to stay in the Mediterranean for a nice warm winter, instead of which they had been hooked back for another winter in the icy Atlantic. Surely the sort of conversation that a group of normal officers might have without, at the time, realizing that they were being insecure (nothing definite being given away) but which even a low grade agent might overhear in a restaurant – and which would be quite substantial confirmation of a whole change of Allied policy when the German Naval Intelligence married it to the other reports.

This example not only illustrates one way in which a deception about a large policy change could be put over but also some of the ways in which the agents could notionally pick up information according to the various jobs that the Germans believed they were doing in order to 'cover' their spying activities and according to their differing characters and life-styles.

5

The Organization of N.I.D. Section 17M

After I had been in the Home Section for about a month, Uncle John sent for me and told me that I was to handle all non-operational Special Intelligence. At that time this, as he told me, consisted mainly of the wireless traffic of the Abwehr – the German Military Intelligence Service under Admiral Canaris which had set up centres (Asts) in the major cities of all the occupied countries and other centres (KOs) in those of many neutral countries.

To get the full picture I was to go down to the deciphering headquarters at Bletchley Park in Buckinghamshire. On no account was I to go in uniform, it was far too secret. Having arrived at Bletchley Junction I asked the taxi-driver to take me to Bletchley Park. 'Oh, the cloak and dagger centre,' he replied – so much for secrecy! There I met a number of people of all backgrounds; many were university professors, some verging on the eccentric – indeed it seemed, possibly falsely, that in many cases the more eccentric you were, the better cryptographer you would be. It was all very fascinating as Denys Page, then an Oxford don, later to be a distinguished professor at Cambridge, and who was certainly not one of the eccentric ones, explained it to me. Some of the cryptographers were near geniuses with the 'hunches' that they got and the belief was (at any rate at that time) that 'an acrostic brain is better at this game than a crossword puzzle brain'.

Most of the Abwehr messages were in transposition ciphers

(the transposing of letters according to set rules, rules which were changed frequently) and these could be deciphered in this way. They varied in complexity (high grade, medium grade and low grade) and the system – at different levels of complexity – continued to be used for run-of-the-mill messages throughout the war, even for some very important messages. Others, especially the most important, were more and more frequently sent in machine ciphers of varying complexity, up to and including the famous Enigma machine. These machine ciphers could only be deciphered by another machine, but it was a bad habit of the Germans that an 'out-station' would report to a large station in a low-grade, fairly easily breakable cipher, and the latter would then pass the identical message on in a higher grade cipher or even in a machine cipher – a habit which might have been designed to help our cryptographers and cryptanalysts – the breakers of ciphers.

At B.P. the two groups worked separately. The breakers of the Enigma machine ciphers produced a steady stream of messages of the highest grade throughout the war. I say a steady stream because from time to time the Germans changed the 'wheels' which enciphered the messages; then there would be a gap in the stream of deciphers produced until they had found the right 'wheels' and combinations of 'wheels' to match this change.

The other group, the one dealing with the non-machine ciphers, also had some inevitable breaks in their production. From time to time the Germans, Japanese and others would change their ciphers, or even their system of ciphers, which might cause a break in the production of the messages which had been sent in those particular ciphers until the brilliant decipherers had broken the new system. The messages deciphered by this group at B.P. varied in importance, some messages being of great value.

It was a most interesting day and I was able to establish personal relationships which were of great help for the rest of the war. It was amusing and instructive to be asked by Denys Page at lunch why I had about me the definite aroma of moth balls. I told him of Uncle John's instructions which had caused me to dig out an old suit of civilian clothes. He roared with laughter and said that the wise precaution was too late – the other Services had not been so secure – in fact D.M.I. had, a week or so before, shown the place off to the Chief of the Imperial General Staff, all the party coming down in full uniform, red tabs, cars flying the Union Flag and all! No wonder the place had earned its local reputation – though, luckily, the actual work that it carried out did not leak to the public, even locally.

Then, in the first weeks of January 1941, Uncle John took me to Wormwood Scrubs prison – at that time the H.Q. of M.I.5 – for the first meeting of the W-Section – soon to be renamed officially the Twenty Committee and, colloquially, the Twenty Club. D.N.I. took the chair and there were represented there, besides the Admiralty, 'C', the War Office, Air Ministry, Home Forces and Home Defence Executive (H.D.E. – the appropriate civilian authority), as well, of course, as M.I.5, whose representatives were Masterman, Lieutenant-Colonel T. A. R. (Tar) Robertson and John Marriott. Of these, Tar Robertson ran Section B.1A and, with John Marriott and a number of extremely able 'case officers', managed the agents and all the day to day work of the double agent system. Masterman – always known by his initials J. C. – chaired the Twenty Committee with supreme tact, equanimity and common sense. They were a brilliant group to whom the country owes much.

The Admiralty had two representatives at that first meeting. My senior officer was Commander Halahan, R.N., but, as he disappeared after the second meeting, I suspected strongly that Uncle John had really brought him to see how things developed in view of the fact that, as usual with an R.N.V.R. officer, I was always one or two ranks lower than my Army colleagues and often two ranks lower than those from the R.A.F. Ours was a good and intelligent committee and I survived through to the 226th and last meeting of the Twenty Committee on 10 May 1945.

But it might not have been so. I knew that J. C. would want to make a check on me, and from experience at Hull I had no great faith in the records of M.I.5. I felt that they were likely to confuse me with my younger and communist brother. I said just that to him over a cup of tea after that first meeting and he

stoutly denied that any check would be made on anyone nomin-
ated by D.N.I. or that their records would be in a muddle. Next
week he asked me, 'How is the table-tennis going?'

I had the joy of replying, 'I said that you would check and
that your records would be in a muddle. That's my communist
younger brother, he's the progenitor of table-tennis, not me.'

However, I soon learnt how different the brain centre of M.I.5
was from those who carried out routine tasks.

I had two facets to my job, Special Intelligence and double
cross. It did not take long to realize how right Uncle John had
been to foresee that it would be invaluable to any officer who
had to try to deceive the German Intelligence, the Abwehr, if
he knew what the Abwehr were already thinking and what other
investigations they were making into a particular subject. It may
seem obvious when stated like that but it is yet another sign of
John Godfrey's instinct for intelligence work that he saw it when
both facets of the work were in embryo, and that none of his
colleagues in either the War Office or Air Ministry ever saw it
even when it had become obvious. My colleagues were always
at a disadvantage, which may have been one of the reasons why
we put over a lot more deceptions about naval matters than
either of the other services did about theirs. They practically
limited themselves, with some notable exceptions, to answering
German questions, often reluctantly and under pressure, and
playing a full part in general strategic deception.

By February 1941 Abwehr messages alone had grown to
twenty-five to thirty a day, many of them abstruse and corrupt,
and we had little 'background' knowledge with which to help
us to interpret what they really indicated. It was too much for
one man, and Dr Joan Saunders (a researcher by profession and
the wife of Hilary Saunders, the author and House of Commons
Librarian) joined me to do filing, indexing and research. We
were moved into our own room in the adjoining corridor, near
Room 39; this was not only because of the Ultra secret nature
of both facets of my duties and of the documents involved. The
embryo group of two became a separate Section 17M.

Various officers and civilians were brought in to help as the
volume of work grew. For the major part of the time, in addi-

tion to Joan Saunders, the main members, to whom the Section is indebted for its achievements, were Marjorie Boxall, my secretary, who also took over the routine burden of filing, Pauline Fenley, Pat Trehearne (a female 'Pat', but she was never known by any other name), Lieutenant-Commander Robin Bartlett, R.N.V.R. (an artist), Lieutenant-Commander Norman Clackson, R.N.V.R. (a yachting journalist who had been serving in the Middle East) who backed me up on the Twenty Committee side, some R.N.V.R. Sub-Lieutenants (including Lieutenant Ken McKay, a New Zealand R.N.V.R. barrister, and Richard Perkins, R.N.V.R.) who acted as watch keepers and were succeeded by W.R.N.S. (Wren) officers (Sally Sullivan and Esme Sherriff), two civilian girls, Patricia Hall and Juliet Ponsonby, and two devoted shorthand typists (Miss McCarthy and Vera Sylvester) who worked long hours often under immense pressure. In addition, Lieutenant-Commander Christopher Shawcross, R.N.V.R. was kept in the general picture of the Special Intelligence in case something happened to me, while Mr E. J. Passant (one of the Foreign Office Librarians) took over this part of the work briefly for me while I was on mission to the United States. In spite of this growth in personnel, the pressure of work became so great that the experiment was made of hiving off the Special Intelligence side which was put under Major Lordon, R.M. to whom I was consultant. However, the division of responsibility did not work out, he was appointed elsewhere and 17M was speedily reconstructed as before. Earlier Lieutenant (S.) Fenley, R.N., and Lieutenant Peer Groves, R.N.V.R. were also with us for a short period.

After a bombing raid our room was moved into the basement of the Admiralty, Room 13, next door to the O.I.C. in the Citadel, otherwise known as Lenin's tomb. Incidentally, while that was being built of thicker and more heavily reinforced concrete than I had ever seen before, I happened to see plans, elevations and sections of the building in the room of one of the Ministers, together with an application under the Building Acts for a licence to erect a *temporary* building!

Our room was far too small, far too cluttered with safes, steel filing cabinets, tables, chairs etc., and especially far too low, with steel girders making it even lower. There was no fresh air, only potted air, and some genius had put the intakes of the system on the lee side of the chimney of the main central heating system so that we collected gallons of soot in our home-made paper deflectors. The only light was, of course artificial. At first everyone worked in their shadows plus the shadows of the girders, but I did manage to get fluorescent lights put in which partially solved that problem in spite of the fact that in those days the tubes flickered almost continuously. There we worked long hours, under pressure, for some four years in conditions which would have been condemned instantly by any factories inspector. We remained practically without illness, I think efficient, and a cheerful and happy group, friends until the present day, thirty years later.

6

Section 17M Gets Under Way

In the early months of 1941 Joan Saunders and I found ourselves gradually gaining an insight into the whole structure of the Abwehr and its out-stations – and a knowledge of many personalities concerned on their side. Indeed, as time went on over the years, we began to regard some almost as friends! Indeed they were often so kind to us unconsciously, that it is not an inapt description.

In our penetration of their activities we were helped immensely by the stupidity of the Germans. They had a delight in using code-names for countries, for places and for people on both their side and ours. This they seemed to believe would make it difficult for the recipient of a deciphered message (or someone on their side who saw a document he should not have seen) to know what it was about. In theory this is a sound idea and would have worked had they applied it as intelligently as we did. *We* allotted all code-names from lists supplied to various commands, at home and abroad, and controlled by the Inter Service Security Board (of which more later). The words on this list could be signalled in one, or very few, groups – which also excluded the names of places, ships and so on – and were chosen so that no deduction could be drawn from them. Examples are: buttercup, cowslip, parsley, mincemeat and so on. Even when Churchill ruled that major operations must be dealt with differently because, as he pointed out, soldiers could not be expected to die for, say, Operation Choc Ice and it would be tragic for a wife to lose her husband in carrying out, say, Operation Pat-a-Cake, he still managed to find neutral words; Torch is not identifiable with North Africa, nor Husky with Sicily; his choice of Overlord for the D-day invasion was probably the most risky.

On the other hand the much vaunted German Intelligence Service regularly called England Golfplatz, and the United States Samland or sometimes Farmland. Even the High Command could not have been more helpful than to use Sealion for the invasion of England! Nevertheless one had to learn this 'language' and keep up to date in it – it was all too easy to get rusty or fall behind changes. Martin was not a person, but the naval section on one service of German stations. It might mean something different on another. Sometimes the code-names were more obscure, but even then the Germans remained helpful. A code-name used on one service, a new one in a changed series, would occur in a signal 'repeated' to another service. The latter would send a signal saying that they could not understand. 'What does so-and-so mean?' And they (and we!) would get the reply, 'It means such and such.' We regretted that we could not send them our thanks!

After a time one could identify different sections of the Abwehr by the names of the addressees or the senders of signals, but one had to be alert for, and remember, changes of the appointments of 'old friends' if they were removed from one station to another.

Over the years 17M got very expert in this technique, but at this time we were only learning. It was fortunate that at this time things were pretty quiet and although we got much of interest from this traffic, nothing very urgent cropped up in it so our expertise had time to grow before it was really put to the test.

Meanwhile, in these early days, the first of my activities which were in themselves of importance were in the double-cross field. I had been appointed secretary of the W-Board but this did not turn out to be in any degree onerous. The Board at first only met about once every three months as and when a policy decision or a decision on a major point of principle was required. Then, as time went on, the W-Board found that they could trust the Twenty Committee, and met at longer and longer intervals, leaving it to their representatives on the Twenty Committee to keep them informed, and the members of the Committee itself to consult individual members of the W-Board when a ruling became necessary. It only had fifteen meetings in all.

But the Twenty Committee was very active. More and more agents were arriving – by parachute, and from neutral ships, and with Polish or other refugee civilians or service men, and a couple even landed in rubber dinghies from a seaplane on the southern shore of the Moray Firth. All were easily picked up. Even if we had not been warned of when and where they were going to arrive (through Special Intelligence) some had badly forged identity cards, one with six mistakes! Some had instructions to make a journey or do something which had been impossible virtually since the outbreak of war. Some had no, or a suspended type of, ration card. Some were so badly trained in English wartime, or even ordinary, habits and slang that they gave themselves away within a few days. One had orders to go to a street that had been bombed months before and, having run out of food and money, committed suicide in an air-raid shelter. It is safe to say that, at least until the end of 1943, no wireless set brought over by a German agent could make contact with occupied Europe until it had been adjusted and improved by M.I.5 experts.

All this inefficiency made us wonder whether it really was due to incompetence or whether such agents were not being planted on us so that the Germans would know that their traffic (as their messages were called) was being controlled by us. Could any intelligence Service, let alone one run by the super-efficient Germans, be so incompetent? We started by playing very safe with the controlled traffic, but gradually checks (especially Special Intelligence) showed us that they were genuine spies and not plants. As the war progressed no degree of incompetence by the Germans surprised us. Indeed we often had to protect them from making bloomers. For instance it is elementary in espionage work that, unless it becomes absolutely essential, one agent (or his group of sub-agents) should not make contact with another (or his group). If that rule is broken and one agent or group gets picked up, the other is almost certain also to be lost.

Again and again we had to persuade the Germans not to make

this error. Our consideration in this respect was not disinterested!
To keep our double-cross work credible it was impossible for a
hundred per cent of the agents to go on for years unscathed and
undetected – so we had from time to time to close down one of
our agents suddenly as if he had been arrested. We certainly did
not want some newly-trained newcomer to be made to report to
one of our best agents whose reputation with the Germans we
had painstakingly built up!

In early 1941 I was mainly engaged, in this part of my job, in
collecting answers to questions on naval matters which had been
asked of the agents and, if one of them had been told to go to,
say, Plymouth or Liverpool, in finding out what he could see
there and be allowed to report.

For this purpose Uncle John had arranged for me to check
with three officers (later a few other Heads of Admiralty Divisions were added) – the Director of Operations Division and his
'Foreign' opposite number and the Director of Plans. These
varied in helpfulness and aptitude for such work, but the Director
of Plans for many years was quite invaluable. He was Captain
Charles Lambe, later to become the First Sea Lord before his
tragically early death. He saw the value of the system, could see
how a ploy might work out and what repercussions for good or
ill it might have. He always appreciated it when one could send
something which was Top Secret at the moment of sending because, by the time it reached the Germans (particularly if the
agent had no wireless set), it would be too late for the Germans
to react to our detriment; and he even would send for me and
offer me something worth having for transmission.

I was collecting material from all these sources. I had also to
consult others who were not 'in the picture'; this had to be done
on some pretext with my real reason 'covered'. Once the information had been obtained a decision had to be made as to what
could be passed, how much of the answer could be true, how
much falsified and how much left out altogether.

At first I was supposed to get approval from the Assistant
Director of Naval Intelligence if anything might impinge on
naval security. This was somewhat time-consuming as A.D.N.I.
was not very bright and everything, literally everything, includ-

ing the purpose of double agent work, had to be explained to him over and over again – but he never took the responsibility of making a decision if he could avoid doing so, and I found a solution to my problem. I took to putting as many requests as possible in writing, always ending: 'I can do either so-and-so or this-and-that. Request instructions.' Almost invariably he wrote 'Approved' and his initial, which gave me a free hand. Eventually he was, for some reason, foolish enough to show one of these documents, with that notation, to Uncle John to get approval of the answer to a follow-up question. Uncle John, of course, realized at once what was happening, was much amused, and told me to take responsibility unless I felt I *needed* advice or approval, and then to come to him or the Deputy Director.

And so we got busier and busier, supplying the answers to questions and building for future deceptions by providing on our own initiative material that the agents might have found out (this we nicknamed 'chicken-feed'), so establishing that various agents notionally had what one might call 'naval connections' (on varying levels) or a chance to pass or visit docks or dock-yards from time to time. The answers and chicken-feed were a mixture of truth, wherever possible, and falsehood where the truth could not be told and where the falsity would not be de-tected or the detection, when it came, would not matter. An example might be the range of some weapon. Here we gained over the other Services as our weapons were less likely to be cap-tured, and if a prisoner-of-war eventually told the truth he might be talking of a later improved weapon or device. Our agents eventually gained such credit with the Abwehr that the Germans believed them and considered the prisoners or other sources to be exaggerating.

One of the first actual deceptions that we put over at this time was one for which C-in-C Home Fleet asked. He write to D.N.I. asking if he could get any misinformation across to the Germans. If so he considered that it might help in any close capital ship action in the northern North Sea, as might happen in the fre-quent very bad visibility, if the Germans believed that King George V class battleships had been fitted with torpedo-tubes.

So we gave one of our pretty-good-level agents a plausible

reason for having to spend a couple of nights in a particular dockyard town, in course of a journey elsewhere, at a time when a K.G. V-class battleship was in fact having a boiler-clean. He reported that he went into a pub, where a torpedo-rating (distinguishable by the badge on his arm) was a bit tight and, in an argument with another rating about how much leave they might get, said that it must take at least a week to fit the torpedo-tubes as such a job was 'not as simple as all that'. This was 'corroborated' to what we felt was a plausible degree by another agent who merely reported that a day or two later he could see a K.G.V. ship in dry-dock from the train as he passed through the town. Further 'corroboration' could have been gained by the Germans from a message from another agent, reporting to the same spy-master, that a man in a train was grousing to a friend that he had lost overtime money as he was missing some shifts while his section of the factory was being altered to produce more torpedoes. It was a useful exercise but we never knew whether it had the slightest effect or even whether it was believed. The next deception, shortly after, was much more interesting and potentially more important.

It was carried out by Tricycle, Dusko Popov, himself. The Germans had approached him to spy for them because they believed he had very high level English contacts. In fact he had once met members of the Royal family when they were holidaying on the Dalmatian Coast. Dusko promptly got in touch with our Embassy, and the Twenty Committee accepted him with joy. On his arrival, via Lisbon, with the cover of starting an import-export and shipping business with Yugoslavia (in a manner which could be of service to the Allies) he was most carefully vetted, especially carefully because that cover would necessitate our allowing him to return from time to time to Lisbon, and thus come into personal contact with the Germans, a difficult and potentially dangerous situation. But he came through that vetting by M.I.5 and the Secret Intelligence Service with flying colours, something that we were never to regret.

Tricycle had brought with him a questionnaire which was of great value in itself and the more so when coupled with his verbal information. One of the things that this *indicated* was that the German invasion was probably postponed. From an intelligent study, and from what he had been told, a delay looked probable, though one could not be sure, and there was no real evidence that it had been abandoned for good.

It occurred to me that, if and when the invasion came, it would be a good thing if we could encourage as many German ships as possible to steer into the east coast mine barrier. This consisted of a series of minefields all the way up the east coast. Naturally, there were many big gaps as we could not produce nor lay enough mines for it to be continuous. The Germans must have had a pretty good idea of *roughly* where the gaps were from reports from their patrolling aircraft who used to watch the fishing trawlers going out to sea and returning. Their findings could only be approximate because it was difficult for aircraft to plot positively precisely with the existing navigational aids.

I therefore suggested that Tricycle should take over to Lisbon a carefully prepared chart in which the minefields would be marked in *slightly* wrong positions calculated not to clash with any positions of trawler channels to a degree which would arouse suspicions. I found that this could be done and a chart was prepared and then 'doctored' so as to indicate considerable use on a chart table such as might have occurred in our H.Q. in the Humber.

When we discussed it with Tricycle we had to consider how to make it plausible. Someone betraying his country for ideological reasons would not be likely to have access to such a document. Someone doing it for money would want payment before he parted with it (even if he trusted Tricycle) and the Germans would not pay the large price which would be needed to make the deal plausible until they had seen the chart (even if *they* trusted Tricycle, who would not have been in a position to check its genuineness). How to get round this impasse?

I suggested the following story to Tricycle. A barrister who had joined the Navy had been stationed at Hull; he had, naturally, been ready to accept the risks of war, but he was a Jew and had heard and believed the propaganda stories about the ill-treatment of Jews and did not want to face the added risk of being handed to the Gestapo if he was captured. He was ready to pass over the chart in return for a 'chit' which would ensure his being handed over to the Abwehr and not the Gestapo. Tricycle liked the story but said that, to be able to put it over successfully, he would have to have some name and details that they could check. 'I thought you had realized, Lieutenant-Commander Montagu,' I said. 'They can look me up in the *Law List* and any of the Jewish Year Books as I'm on many charity committees and so on.' He was satisfied. The idea had the merit of 'guaranteeing' the genuineness of the chart as, if it was phoney, any 'chit' that I produced to a German captor would be my death warrant.

I hasten to disclaim any pretensions to courage. The odds against my now being put in a position where I could be captured with my Ultra secret knowledge were astronomic and the last thing that I would have done if the miracle had occurred would be to use the 'chit'.

In the event the deal went through, but our subsequent check-ups do not suggest that the Germans valued the chart very highly although they accepted it as genuine. Their lack of interest was probably due to the invasion being 'off'. I never collected the 'chit' from Section B.1A but I got a bit worried, after we had won the war, about what would happen if the chart and its documentation turned up among the captured German archives. While no prosecution would take place, the discovery of the chart and name of its supplier would not have seemed to be secret at the time of discovery and could well leak, and any attempt to explain that away publicly would definitely have been security-barred!

At about this time we took the first steps in what developed into a long-term, sustained, naval deception. In more than one of the questionnaires given to agents whom the Germans sent over there were instructions to find out anything that they could about our radar, radar research and any development that we might be hoping for in that field.

I consulted Captain Lambe, and a brilliant young scientist, Professor Gollin, who was N.I.D.'s adviser on all scientific matters. They felt that it would be to our advantage if the Germans were led to believe that the range of our radar, then and in the foreseeable future, was less than it was. Arguments could be advanced for the view that, if we took the opposite course and exaggerated our radar, it would make the Germans more anxious at night and in bad weather conditions, if they believed that we could spot them before they could spot us. So Captain Lambe got the views of various senior officers, including some serving at sea. This he did with great skill without revealing why he wanted the information, indeed often being able to conceal what exactly it was that he was trying to find out. The great preponderance of opinion supported the view that we should keep the range as low as was plausible. From then on we kept the range at that of at least one model behind our latest one. This would protect our agents from being blown if a captured ship, or talkative prisoner, revealed a longer range than we had reported – our agent would merely not have got particulars of the latest model, although he had been accurate about the one before.

I might mention here that, later on, it was our experts who asked us to pass misinformation on this subject, instead of our having to seek from them enough of a directive for us to be able to answer plausibly the questions that the Germans were putting to us. As I will mention in due course, we were asked to be specific about wave-lengths.

Section B.1A were, of course, managing the notional life of the agents and we manoeuvred one or two of the agents who had been asked questions about radar into situations and relationships from which they could pick up bits of relevant information. To maintain plausibility others had of course to be unable to answer the questions. In addition, other agents who had not been specifically asked but who were in situations where they might pick up information about radar, reported bits and pieces. I say bits and pieces because, obviously, no agent could hope to be able to provide a full report on radar and its capabilities – so Professor Gollin produced a mass of little bits of information which might be picked up by someone in a certain place, or which might be leaked in the hearing of someone with the right friends, a series which taken together would convey the picture that we wanted. Then, when there was a chance of manoeuvring a particular agent into the right place or circle of friends Gollin and I would discuss which bits of information he should pick up, sometimes, for the sake of plausibility, giving one part of one bit and one part of another. Then I had to consult with Tar Robertson, and perhaps also the appropriate case officer working the agent, as to whether it would be 'in character' for a particular agent to put over a message in that particular form, or whether we should either alter it or give that agent a different 'bit' and manoeuvre another agent into a position where *he* could pick up and transmit the 'bit' that we had in mind.

It occupied a great deal of time and energy but it was fascinating work. In a way it was like a mixture of constructing a crossword puzzle and sawing a jig-saw puzzle and then waiting to see whether the recipient could and would solve the clues and place the bits together successfully, except that it was *we* who would get the prize if the recipient succeeded. We had no illusions about the efficiency of the German Abwehr, so we had to make sure that the puzzle was not too difficult for them to solve!

This particular exercise lasted for some years. After some of the naval actions during the North Russian convoys and the chase of the *Bismarck*, we learnt from Special Intelligence that the Germans were surprised by the range at which we detected them and the accuracy of our radar-controlled firing. When we captured the German Naval Archives at the end of the war we learnt that the Germans had informed their fleet that our radar had exactly the (lesser) range that we had intended that they should deduce. Indeed, the Chief of German Naval Operations, Admiral Meisel, had gone so far on 21 February 1944 as to attribute the loss of the *Scharnhorst* quite specifically to this belief that the range of our radar was less than it actually was. This deception operation was a complete success.

The co-operation with Professor Gollin was very fruitful. He had a broad scientific knowledge and an alert and ingenious mind. While he readily appreciated the advantage of either leading the Germans astray about our research and development, or causing them to embark on a path which could have no useful end result, he was alert to see that we did not give them an idea which might usefully be developed. Also he was able to see that some item labelled Secret *must* inevitably be known also to German scientists and, in spite of its classification, could safely be 'discovered' and passed on by our double agents. Much of it was well above my head, but when checks were made after the war there was some indication of successes and no indication at all that he had made the mistake of helping the Germans.

We owed much to Professor Gollin's help, but my only experience with another, much more famous, scientist was far less happy. I think that it was at about this time that Uncle John sent for me to say that I was to go and see Professor Lindemann, Winston Churchill's adviser, and later Lord Cherwell, as he had sent a note to D.N.I. to say that he had a scheme for deceiving the enemy which he would like to explain.

The 'Prof' (as he was always known) outlined his scheme. It was that we should mislead the German meteorologists by placing buoys, which reported the weather by wireless, in the Bay of Biscay, Channel and North Sea. These would be so adjusted that they gave false barometric and wind reports. We would ignore them, but, if the 'cipher' in which they reported was breakable, the Germans would get their forecasts wrong.

I was astounded that a man of his intellect should put up so fatuous a proposal. I replied that the scheme might work for a couple of days at most, after which the weather reaching the Germans would show incontrovertibly that the buoys were bogus – indeed it could well be that the Germans would soon be able to make in the calculations the same adjustments as we had made to the buoys – and thus gain benefit from the scheme.

Then came the revelation of what the Prof was up to. Casually he asked, 'Talking of a cipher that the Germans could break, I suppose that Naval Intelligence, as in the last war, are breaking German ciphers?' I kept my head and replied, 'Not as far as I know, sir – and I should have thought that I would know if we were doing it.'

He asked some more questions on this topic and got similar answers, and I realized why so brilliant a man had put forward so obviously futile a scheme and why he had offered it to the Navy, rather than to the R.A.F. who could so much more easily have laid such buoys.

When I reported to D.N.I. and reached the Prof's question, he nearly exploded and burst in with, 'I hope you kept your head.' I told him my reply which seemed to satisfy him, but he remained furious at this attempt to go behind his back and 'pump' a junior officer.

Another long-term naval deception concerned shipbuilding. We naturally decided to send over messages which would add up to a higher rate of building than was, in fact, being achieved. Again post-war research indicated that we had had a considerable degree of success. And the naval shipbuilding side of this deception helped us to put over a quite important deception later on.

These naval deceptions were, of course, in addition to the traffic that was being passed over on a vast number of other matters with which I was not personally concerned, except as a member of the Twenty Committee. Such things as a general uplift of manufacture of ammunition, aircraft, tanks etc., and little bits which would cause the Germans to consider that we had more trained soldiers than we in fact had.

Meanwhile the Special Intelligence was beginning to pour in. At first it continued to be predominantly Abwehr messages which were mainly of what one might call security or counter-espionage interest – apart, of course, from the invaluable checks that they provided on whether our double agents' messages were being accepted and passed on by their spy-masters at the K.O.s in Spain and Portugal and the Ast. in Paris, with a double-check by way of the comments and replies from Berlin.

At this period information on impending arrivals of Abwehr agents in this country and in Iceland in small boats from France or Norway, pretending to be refugees, was particularly helpful in the delicate process of separating the sheep from the goats among such persons. K.O. Madrid once even helped us to pick up an agent sent by yacht from Spain to West Africa!

Several attempts were made (and notified to us) to land agents from U-Boats in the Mediterranean area. Special Intelligence signals on this sort of subject were often sufficiently urgent to be regarded as 'operational', in which case the messages would be teleprinted direct to the O.I.C. to whom 17M would give background information to help their consideration of whether action could be taken.

The reports from agents in Spain and Portugal, to their superiors in Madrid and Lisbon, and passed on by them to Berlin (and us), revealed what they had learned from seamen visiting those ports, so we had a check, which lasted throughout the war, on what 'gossip' was leaking through this unstoppable gap. It sometimes also revealed definite espionage by seamen or purported seamen and it was Special Intelligence that started investigations which led to the capture, conviction and execution in 1942 of one man as a traitor, and this in turn led to better countermeasures.

In addition we learned of at least a hundred Spanish and some Portuguese ships in which there were agents who reported, sometimes while at sea but usually on return to port, what they had seen in their ports of call and on passage. Some were individually identified, while others were identified only by their jobs – officers, W/T operators, stewards and so on. This knowledge was somewhat frustrating as it was usually impossible to take positive action without compromising our far too valuable source. But they could, at any rate, usually be put on the blacklist through A.D.N.I.

There was also revealed to us the problem of the subornation by the Germans of members of the crews of neutral fishing-vessels, and we started to accumulate evidence to identify the trawlers and justify action.

Finally, as regards the counter-espionage angle at this stage of the war, we were beginning to accumulate evidence of the great extent of German espionage and ship-reporting in the Gibraltar area, in which the Germans were so ably and enthusiastically backed by Spanish officers, officials and Ministers.

Quite apart from all this information of counter-intelligence value, we were receiving an ever increasing flow of straight intelligence. A number of Abwehr and other stations in the Aegean and Greek Islands were sending excellent and informative reports, which we, of course, also received. These for a very long time constituted virtually our only information from those areas.

Gradually both the Special Intelligence and deception work

grew and grew, many individual facets of each developing over a long period and, of course, overlapping one another.

As to my personal life at this period, my wife and I managed to write to one another at least once a week. We numbered our letters and kept carbon copies so that we could each trace what points the other was answering in spite of letters arriving in no particular order. I could, of course, say nothing which could even hint at my work.

Our correspondence therefore consisted of our feelings, family matters and, on my side, my non-working life. I thus have a detailed record of those subjects. Of the feelings the only matters relevant to this story, as they influenced other matters, were the inevitable misery of separation and my being deprived of watching the two children in the fascinating period of their growing up from the ages of nine and twelve. The letters are full of that, and it is interesting to see 'between the lines' how the interest and pressure of my work managed to keep my morale up, in spite of two somewhat depressing events in this period.

The lesser one was that, in March 1941, the Admiralty decided that marriage and children's allowances were 'payable for the current maintenance of wife and children' so I found that my remuneration was down by 52s. 6d. a week in spite of the fact that many of the expenses of a family man were continuing. Almost simultaneously, Uncle John's first attempt to get me promoted one step nearer many of my opposite numbers on various committees failed.

The second was more important. I got a letter from the India Office to say that there would soon be need to replace two of the Chief Justices in India, one in Bombay and the other in Madras. I had been recommended by one of the Lord Justices in England whom they had consulted and, if I was interested in the Chief Justiceship of Bombay, would I call. I did so and the discussion was interesting.

There were many points for and against. Even if the Admiralty were to let me go (which I doubted) there was the uprooting from a life at the Bar which I thoroughly enjoyed, separation from friends, and, although my wife would be with me and, indeed, we might well be together far sooner than if I stayed in the Navy, there would still be much separation from the children. On the other hand, the work sounded interesting, I had always been fascinated by India since my Uncle Edwin had been Secretary of State, and I would see the working out of the Montagu-Chelmsford Reforms. I had many Indian friends from Cambridge days, and there was the security of a salary as against the great difficulty of successfully re-starting a practice which had been abandoned for years less than six months after taking silk.

I had to decide this with only time for one letter to, and one letter from, my wife. In the end I decided that I would leave it to fate. I told the India Office that I would accept an offer, if made, but would not myself apply for release from the Navy. If the India Office decided they wanted me it was up to them to convince the Admiralty that their need was more important even in war time. The officer smiled and said that he didn't foresee any difficulty. He was probably comparing in his mind the responsibilities of a Chief Justice and a Lieutenant-Commander R.N.V.R. He didn't know the Admiralty system. Whether, in the end, they decided to approach the Admiralty or dropped the whole idea I will never know.

There was another period of anxiety towards the end of July when I got a 'bug' in my eyes and suddenly almost lost my eyesight. I was put into the Royal Masonic Hospital at Ravenscourt Park. The very real anxiety whether I was going to go blind was soon dispelled and what a wonderful hospital it was!

Apart from that hospital break I got two leaves, a week at Christmas (before work really got going) and a week in June. The first I spent (after Christmas and Boxing Day with my sister and brother-in-law at their house at Ogbourne St George) on Exmoor with Sir Robert Waley-Cohen, and the second also on Exmoor at Withypool with my great friends Vernon and Angela Sainsbury. We were fishing the game little trout and staying at the then unspoiled but very comfortable pub, the Royal Oak. I say unspoiled because, except for the comfortable beds and good food and a 'rod-room' opening to the road, it was a 'local'. The customers all came on horseback or by cycle, and they came from miles around as the beer came from a little

Somerset brewery where it was all hand-brewed. Indeed it was so good that Harold, the road-mender, lived almost solely on it; he spent practically all his meagre pay on it, rather than on solid food, and spent in the same way the money he won at shove-ha'penny on the lovely old table in the bar. He was a brilliant player and, as the evenings wore on and the beer took hold, he 'timed his sways' perfectly and played better and better to the consternation of those who felt that at this stage they might get their money back. At closing time he would go out and sleep under a nearby hedge. We were told that he did that in all weathers. *Real* beer is good for you!

Apart from those two leaves I had a day off most weeks. We arranged our rota for this by mutual consent. When we fixed the rota there was a little bickering, but I pointed out that we were all of us grown-up and that it was much better that we should do it by give-and-take where necessary than that I should write a rota out, as head of the Section, which would probably suit no one. I was glad to find that, in the rapidly resulting agreement, I could sometimes have Saturdays and sometimes Sundays, which meant that I could quite frequently get down to Ogbourne St George for a breath of fresh air, peace and quiet and the joys of a happy household in perfect surroundings.

Apart from that it was very hard work for long hours, a situation for which I was luckily prepared by pre-war days at the Bar. I was usually in the office well before 9 a.m. so as to check the Orange Summary (see Chapter 9) before it was circulated and I could take it to D.N.I. for him to see in case he was rung up by the First Sea Lord with a question about it; more frequently, however, I was rung direct if there was any query. Then there was a steady flog for the rest of the day. This might include a meeting of the Twenty Committee, or of the Inter Service Security Board or of some other inter-Service or ad hoc committee. Each day D.N.I. had a meeting, nicknamed by those not entitled to be present 'The Pets' Get-Together'. Here the members of his personal staff and the heads of most of the Sections and I, that is to say all entitled to see Special Intelligence in its original form, reported anything which he felt might help the others to know, and Uncle John directed the discussion and initiated any resulting action.

The only break was about half an hour for lunch which I usually had at the snack-bar of the United Services Club, which had made many of us honorary members and which was very near. One day, as we crossed from the North West door of the Admiralty and were passing Admiralty Arch, the Home Guard sentry there (a private) saluted my companion Captain 'Ginger' Lewis. Ginger returned the salute and said, with a smile, 'Good morning, sir.' When I asked the reason, Ginger said, 'Didn't you notice the ribbon of the K.C.B.? That was Admiral Sir . . .' Duly chastened, I adopted Ginger's very proper practice to the obvious pleasure of the distinguished veteran.

Usually I would get home to Kensington Court by about 7 p.m. but sometimes there was a flap on, or just a vast amount of work to do, and I would not be able to leave the Admiralty until 10 p.m. or even later. Naturally this would be likely to happen if I had fixed up to dine with someone or go to a cinema or theatre.

The one thing I missed, apart from Iris and the family, was exercise. During Ogbourne week-ends I could walk on the Marlborough downs, but otherwise it was hard to come by. Virtually all I got was the cycle ride to M.I.5, who had moved to the top of St James's Street, where I went for the Twenty Committee and for other discussions, and to the Secret Intelligence Service by St James's Park Underground Station or another office of theirs in Ryder Street, St James's.

At first I wondered about cycling as I usually had to have with me a big brief-case which contained super secret papers (either Special Intelligence or about double agents). This problem I solved by fixing a large metal basket-type carrier to the front of the cycle. To this I chained the brief-case with the padlock and chain with which I locked the cycle when it was parked. There was some doubt about the security of the operation for such 'hot' documents, but I managed to get permission to adopt it as long as I always wore a shoulder-holster and automatic pistol.

7

Mission to America

During this year of 1941 it was steadily becoming more and more apparent that double agent work was going to be of great value. Not only were we gaining short term advantages, but the Germans were showing that they valued the agents highly, and we had growing reason to be confident that we would be able to retain complete control of information reaching the enemy from this country. This we were achieving by satisfying them that 'their' spy system was working well and sending reports that they could trust, even if they conflicted with reports from neutral diplomats and occasional informants. Also we would be able to use the agents under our control to deceive the enemy, not only on minor but also on major matters. Our special aim from the start was to deceive them on what would be the all important matter of con-cealing essential facts about the inevitable invasion of Europe. We were determined to try to ensure that the enormous confidence that the Germans showed in Tate and Tricycle especially should be preserved and, if possible, increased right up to that eventual return to Europe.

Tate had been parachuted into England in September 1940 and when he was duly picked up, he confessed under interrogation and agreed to work for us. After some low-level reporting by wire-less at the start of his career, he in fact became ill and an M.I.5 wireless operator successfully imitated his transmission style. As this was not spotted by the Germans we did not want to risk another change of style and Tate did not himself transmit again.

He became our most valued wireless agent, sending really high
level information to Hamburg from October 1940 until twenty-
four hours before that city fell in May 1945. Not only did we
value him highly but the Germans gave him the Iron Cross, both
First and Second class, having specially naturalized him for that
purpose, a rare compliment.

The German belief in Tate's value to them at this time was
not only shown by the traffic of messages between him and Hamburg but was confirmed by the enormous trouble to which the
Germans went to keep him paid. Payment of their agents was
always a source of difficulty for the Germans and, of course, for
us, because, if the Germans could not keep our agents in funds,
they could not plausibly continue to operate.

The efforts by the Germans to get money to Tate at this period
illustrates this general proposition. Snow, another useful double
agent, who had actually been recruited before the war, had visited
Lisbon and came back with £10,000 in addition to sabotage
material (including explosive fountain pens) of considerable
interest to our security people. This money was none too much to
provide for his own activities and those of his mainly imaginary
group, but the Germans took the risk (contrary to careful spy-
management) of getting him to send £100, which he could ill
spare, by registered post to Tate to keep the latter going until
further funds could be provided.

Next, detailed arrangements were made for £500 to be dropped
to Tate by aeroplane, but these could not be implemented. Then
'a friend' was to meet Tate through a series of meetings at the
Regent Palace Hotel, the Tate Gallery (the Germans did not
know how appropriate this was for *our* code-name for him!) and
the British Museum. None of these rendezvous were kept for some
reason we never learned. Tate reported this, and that he was getting impatient. Then another 'friend' failed to make contact, a
failure for which, in one sense, he couldn't be blamed as that
friend was a man named Richter who managed to get himself
arrested – and eventually executed – fortunately with no compromising contact with Tate.

After all these abortive efforts the Germans must have been
becoming desperate. Eventually they came up with a scheme

which seemed to us to have been drawn direct from a spy-novel and we began to wonder whether Richter's arrest might not, after all, have blown Tate. He was told to go to Victoria on a particular day, wait until 1600 hrs. and then get on to the next No. 11 bus at its terminus. A Japanese with a book and *The Times* in his left hand would get on also, Tate would get off at the fifth stop, as would the Japanese. Both would then get on to the next bus and there they would exchange pre-arranged remarks and the Japanese would give Tate his newspaper which would contain money. Tate just had time before the date fixed to warn the Germans that No. 11 buses had no terminal at Victoria and to suggest a No. 16 instead. The rendezvous was watched, everything went according to plan, Tate got £200, and the Japanese rather naively went back – to the Japanese embassy! He turned out to be one of the Assistant Naval Attachés.

Had the go-between been a member of the Spanish embassy, we would not have been really surprised, though, even then, such blatant use of a neutral diplomat, with its risk of an 'incident', would have shown some degree of desperation and that they believed in Tate and valued him highly. To use a Japanese diplomat in the first half of 1941 was indeed an accolade.

At about the same time, early in 1941, Tricycle was involved in a scheme that we called Plan Midas, which we devised so as to help the Germans over their difficulties in making payments to their (and our!) agents. He told the Germans in Lisbon that he had been asked if he could smuggle a large sum to Lisbon, and there change it into dollars. His story was that the suggestion had been made by a theatrical agent, a Jew, who thought that England would lose the war and wanted to smuggle his money to America, to which country he hoped to go. Tricycle suggested that he should play safe, hand the money to someone in England (or get the theatrical agent to do so) and the Germans should give him the dollars in Lisbon. After referring to Berlin for instructions, the Abwehr arranged that the theatrical agent should pay £20,000 to Tate, whom they instructed to collect it. They then paid the equivalent in dollars to Tricycle in Lisbon. Perhaps 'equivalent' is not quite the right word, as a not inconsiderable rake-off was retained by the Abwehr officers there.

This sudden affluence of Tate put us in difficulty. He was very able and very personable, and the Germans suggested that he should now be able to cultivate rich and influential friends and also to get about the country. Section B.1A countered by having him (in his report) nearly called-up for military service, so he reported that he had got a responsible job on a farm. This enabled *us* to decide when he could get away for a journey or when he could get up to London to 'socialize'. At this comparatively un-eventful period of the war we would otherwise have had difficulty in providing him with enough information on his customarily high level to keep the Germans happy.

Meanwhile there were developments in Tricycle's situation. When the Germans invaded Yugoslavia they had had doubts as to his loyalty to them – but, ever the actor, Tricycle persuaded them that, as a *Serb*, he was not violently pro-Yugoslavia as an entity, and that he was willing to continue to work for the Germans as long as they did not ask him to do anything against any of the nations which had formed that group. Although the Germans accepted this they felt that his 'cover' job in England could not last long in the new situation. So he was asked to go to America, having first recruited at least two agents in England to carry on, as well as they could, in his absence.

America, although still neutral, was of course helping Britain in many ways, and the Germans wanted to get information about supplies of all sorts which were being sent to England, the sailing of ships and convoys, the building of Liberty ships, and the repair of warships in the States. But most of all, Tricycle was told, they wanted him to build up a completely new high-level spy network over there, with an especial view to the likelihood of America joining the war on the Allied side. Most of what they already had in the States was founded on the large numbers of German-Americans who had, so far, shown themselves very inept and were also bound to be known to, and easy meat for, the F.B.I. im-mediately war broke out. Tricycle was to go his own way and on no account to make any contact with any existing group. He would not be told of them, nor they of him.

The Twenty Committee considered this proposal most carefully in consultation with 'C', the Secret Intelligence Service. A dominant factor was that it would be difficult for Tricycle to find a plausible reason for refusing to go. On the other hand we did not want to lose the very high-level deception channel that he could provide both currently and, we hoped, when the invasion of Europe took place. Nor did we want to lose the valuable information that he brought back from his visits to Lisbon and, occasionally, to Madrid, as well as the flow of similarly valuable information that we could deduce from his questionnaires and instructions. Again, in favour of his going to America, if that country *did* come into the war, we could gain much if there were a high-level spy network in America under Allied control. A final argument for his going was that 'C' stressed that it would greatly increase co-operation with the F.B.I. if we could hand over to them a ready-made possibility of their controlling a first-class German spy network. So after discussions between 'C' himself and J. Edgar Hoover, the head of the F.B.I., it was decided that Tricycle should agree to the German's wishes. He went back to Lisbon and thence flew to the States.

We immediately gained a very great bonus. Recent messages in Special Intelligence had from time to time contained references to something they called 'Micropunkt' and, while we had suspicions, we were not certain what this actually was. To our joy Tricycle's instructions and questionnaire were contained in micropunkts – which turned out literally to be microdots, a minute dot the size of a full stop in a printed or typewritten document.

Even to a non-scientist like myself the process involved was explicable in a general way. You took any document up to a whole sheet of closely typed foolscap. You photographed it through a camera that was what one might call a *reversed* high powered microscope, on to a special film which had virtually no 'grain'. The result was a small, shiny full-stop from which could be read, through a microscope used in the ordinary way, the text of a whole long document!

News of this means of conveying instructions, questionnaires or, worse still, reports, was terrifying to our security people. They now had an awe-inspiring problem. Any letter, any book, any newspaper, any magazine carried by a traveller in his belongings or sent through the post, could contain, in each of any one or more full stops in the text, a whole sheet of writing – for the microdot could be stuck on the top of any full-stop in the document. The only way in which it could be discovered was by carefully twisting the document about while slanting it against the light – so that one could see that it was shiny. Think of doing that to every page of every book, every letter or magazine that a traveller had with him, and of doing it to every letter at a censorship station! And it did not end there. The microdot could be fixed to any object – the inside of a suitcase, the inside of a shirt collar or of a folded handkerchief. The possibilities were endless and the potential dangers to security were immense. The only limiting factor to the danger was that, for a *spy* to use it to report, he would have to have the delicate and complex camera and special film involved. Fortunately, as we knew from Special Intelligence, the Germans were not in a position to supply these essentials to many spies.

Tricycle's mission revealed much more of great value. First, there was what was *in* the microdots. His instructions revealed, apart from other matters of great interest, that an urgent priority was for him to go, as soon as he could, to Hawaii, and his questionnaire contained many questions about Pearl Harbor – the answers to which could only be of interest to the Japanese. We knew from Special Intelligence how Hitler was courting the Japanese and trying to do them favours, and this married in with a verbal report from Tricycle that his friend, the senior official in the Abwehr who had originally recruited him as an agent, had just recently helped a high ranking naval member of a special Japanese mission to Berlin to go on a visit to Italy, which they regarded as being vitally important. The purpose of this visit was to get information, which the Japanese by themselves could not get from the Italians, about all the highly secret details of the British raid on Taranto, the successful raid in which Italian warships were sunk by naval aircraft, flown off from an aircraft carrier well off-shore. Taken together, the questionnaire and this report formed a strong indication that, to put it no higher, the

Japanese might try a surprise raid of this kind on Pearl Harbor, and they wanted the background intelligence *urgently*.*

When the offer of Tricycle's services had been made to Hoover, 'C' had briefed him fully and given him a complete picture of Dusko Popov's background character and way of life – and how he would have to continue to live a 'playboy' type of life if the Germans were not to deduce immediately that he had been caught and was operating under control, but that this would not cost the American taxpayer a cent as the Germans were providing him with 40,000 dollars, and could be made to continue to provide more. He was told how completely we trusted Dusko Popov in his role as Tricycle, how his reports had always been accurate and how we had been able to deduce many of the German's intentions from his questionnaires. Hoover had also been told of Tricycle's general instructions not to contact any other German agent but to found a new and better network against the day when Hoover and his F.B.I. mopped up existing agents.

We in the Twenty Committee were naturally confident that Tricycle would be welcomed on reaching America, would be allowed to report his safe arrival and arrangements for living and for getting his cover occupation safely established and to send over intelligence reports – naturally minor at first, but increasing in value as would happen in real life.

Tricycle arrived in New York in the second week of August 1941, almost four months before Pearl Harbor. To our horror we learned that Hoover's actual management of Tricycle could not have been more calculated to blow him if Hoover had sat down to devise and plan a method of doing so. He was met by junior officials to whom he had to re-explain everything (including the microdot†) – neither Hoover nor anyone senior interviewed him for more than a fortnight and then, when Tricycle forced a meeting, Hoover exploded at him that he would not tolerate

---

* If any reader has any doubt about this statement they can find Tricycle's questionnaire set out in full in an Appendix in Sir John Masterman's book, *The Double Cross System*. When coupled with the Japanese special interest in the raid on Taranto it seems incredible that Pearl Harbor should not have been on the alert for a surprise hit-and-run air raid *if* Hoover had not failed to pass on what Tricycle had brought him.

† In 1946 Hoover, in an article in *Reader's Digest,* claimed to have captured a spy and, brilliantly, discovered the microdot.

Tricycle's extravagant and playboy way of life and that, not only was he not a grade one agent, he wasn't even a mediocre one as no German agent had even attempted to make contact with him.

We at once got 'C' to try to persuade Hoover to implement his promise to work Tricycle properly, or at least send him back (Tricycle would have found some plausible excuse for the Germans) but even Sir William Stephenson (always known as 'Little Bill'), the brilliant Head of our Security Co-ordination in America who had established such invaluable co-operation with Hoover, could not persuade him to do anything worth while. Hoover the policeman obviously only regarded Tricycle as potential fly-paper which other agents would approach, and so get caught – and imprisoned with all possible publicity. For this purpose, Hoover did at least keep Tricycle 'alive', albeit with pathetically low-level, trumpery reports, wholly out of character with the able working that the Germans had grown to expect from Tricycle, while Tricycle himself was getting more and more frustrated. The luxurious life that he was living was not his real aim and he saw all that he had done being thrown away. Soon he threatened to throw the whole thing up and join the fighting forces.

Something *had* to be done. One of 'C's' senior men who had been a member of the Twenty Committee was sent over to re-inforce Sir William Stephenson's arguments, but the latter warned us that it was always a long job to get Hoover to alter a set course, *if* one could achieve that. So the Twenty Committee decided that I should go over, if D.N.I. would allow it, and set up a mini-Twenty Committee in Washington. This would consist of one selected officer from each Service in the Missions in Washington who would provide reasonably high-grade Service information which Tricycle could send over if Hoover would let him. Tricycle could use as an explanation a story that he had no ready-made contacts with Americans, such as he had in English 'society', and was finding it difficult for a Yugoslav newcomer to make worth while contacts, even in his notional cover job as a member of the Yugoslav information mission. However he had met an officer in the British mission whom he had known in London and through him had met others. This, we felt, could keep him 'alive' for a time while Hoover was worked on.

The choice fell on me partly because, owing to Uncle John's having seen the need for the officer who did Double Cross work also to see all Special Intelligence, I had perhaps done rather more in the Twenty Committee than my Service colleagues. But the main reason was that I had met and formed a friendship with Dusko Popov. It was, very rightly, not the practice for members of the Twenty Committee, other than the B.1A representatives, to meet or even know the real names of our agents unless it was essential for some reason – indeed, throughout the war, I only met one other double agent, Zigzag, who was to appear later.

Uncle John was reluctant to let me go, but was persuaded of the necessity and eventually agreed. I left, after indoctrinating Mr Passant to carry on with 17M. My orders from Uncle John showed the other side of the character of that strange genius – a side that is hard to believe. I reminded him that my wife and family were in the States, that I hadn't seen them for eighteen months and wouldn't see them again for years, pointed out that I had a leave owing me and asked if I might have a week in Boston, where they were, after my job had been completed.

Uncle John said, 'I've agreed to let you have the fortnight in Washington and New York which your job will need. You'll arrive about December 4 or 5 and there is a passage back on December 21 from Halifax which I've arranged that you'll take. If you miss that sailing, you'll be court-martialled.' As I once wrote to my wife, I'd always prefer to work for a . . . than a fool.' One always felt that working for Uncle John was well worth while, but this order was hard to forgive!

I sailed in the French liner *Pasteur* from the Clyde in late November 1941. On arrival in Halifax I sent a telegram to my wife in Boston. Although on her arrival in the States she had been required to sign a form undertaking that, as she was being allowed in as a 'refugee', she would not take paid employment, it was later discovered that she had in fact been admitted 'on the quota' by mistake and could therefore ignore that form 'which was not applicable', in the words of the authorities. Her kind hostess, Mrs Bancroft, could not have been more hospitable, but it was embar-

rassing not have a penny of her own, even to buy Mrs Bancroft or
any of the family a present. Our daughter Jennifer was attending
a public (in the American definition) school in Boston and another
old friend, the always incredibly generous Howard Goodhart of
New York, had sent our son Jeremy to a private (in the American
definition) boarding school, Hotchkiss in Connecticut, where the
education would be of more use to him when he got home. So Iris,
having free time most of the year, had taken a job as reception
hostess at a sea-food restaurant in Cohasset, where the Bancrofts
spent the summer, and then as a hat-and-coat-check-girl at the
Puritan Hotel in Boston when the family returned there. When
she heard that I was coming she had got her boss's permission
for the job to be taken over by a friend for the length of my visit,
and Howard Goodhart offered to put us up in a room near his
suite at the St Regis Hotel in New York for any period that we
were there. Finally, through the English Speaking Union, Iris had
arranged that we could both have the kind hospitality of Mr and
Mrs James Oliver Murdoch during my stay in Washington. We
were to meet in New York, where I was to stay two nights so as
to contact Security Co-ordination, and then fly on to Washington.

From Halifax I travelled to Montreal, and thence to New York.
I realized I was in another world, or another age. After years of
total blackout, I saw lights again – no blinds to pull down on the
train and lights shining everywhere as I journeyed on.

I arrived in New York on a Saturday, just in time to contact
Sir William Stephenson and to learn that nothing could be gained
by reaching Washington before Monday, as everyone on this side
of the Atlantic was still on peace-time routine. So after a joyous
reunion with Iris, we decided to take the train out to Hotchkiss on
Sunday to see Jeremy.

We took him by taxi to the local restaurant to which,
apparently, all visiting parents took their sons for a steak lunch.
When we came out the taxi-driver said that he was keeping his
radio on. 'They're putting out some programme like that one
about the Martians invading the earth that fooled everybody –
something about the little yellow-bellies bombing Pearl Harbor.'

The train back to New York was full of returning week-enders, none of whom had radios or papers, so the rumour remained unsubstantiated when we arrived at Grand Central Station. There we had a snack at the excellent bar-restaurant. Still no one seemed certain until a very drunken American 'gob', or naval rating, seeing my uniform, staggered over, flung his arm round my neck, shoved a cigar in my mouth, and said, 'Thank God we're buddies again!' Thus I learnt that England had a new ally.

Next morning Iris and I went to La Guardia airport. We were told that all flights were cancelled as enemy air raids on Washington were thought to be imminent. Then we were told that our flight could just make it before Washington airport was closed down, but we would be restricted to a very low altitude.

In Washington the Murdochs couldn't have been kinder and more hospitable and we enjoyed our stay. Work was not pressing and I walked to the Embassy Annexe each morning with the Chief Justice of the Supreme Court, who lived near the Murdochs and was one of those rare Americans who actually liked walking. Iris had recently taken a pair of shoes back to the shop to complain that the soles had worn through in less than a month and the assistant, having looked at the soles, handed them back with the scornful remark, 'You've walked in them.'

I got the mini-Twenty Committee organized and Iris and I returned to New York I saw Tricycle before leaving for home, who true to the image that he had to keep up, was living in an apartment that he had taken with German money, a lovely penthouse in ultra fashionable Park Avenue. For the only time in our friendship – which extends to the present day – I found him depressed and worried, with all that gaiety which exudes from him completely gone.

The explanation was easy. He burst out, 'I'm no fool – I realize that just because Colonel Robertson and you say I'm O.K. the Americans need not believe it – they are right to check me – but they are such fools – such incompetents – when I smell the flowers I scratch my nose on a microphone in the vase – when I adjust a cushion, there's a microphone – microphones everywhere – these G-men, for moscles they are vonderful, but for brains, "Pfui"!'

It was the first and only time that I've heard that expression spoken – it was pronounced just as it is spelled.

I explained to him what I had been able to fix up, but he realized as well as I did that it was pretty futile, unless Hoover could be persuaded to play, which did not seem likely. But I think that my mission and visit to him were really worth while – when one has regard to Tricycle's service to us in the rest of the war – because of the boost that they gave to his morale. It persuaded him that there *were* people who still believed in him, that we were ready to go to real trouble to keep him 'alive' as a double agent, that we still wanted to use him and, from his point of view, to enable him to continue his work against the Nazis for which he had risked his life on each visit to Lisbon, as he was to risk it again, more than once.

Nothing would move Hoover – it is hard to know why. He couldn't or wouldn't see the value of deception of the enemy. I suppose it was because he was really just a policeman and just good at catching people. There was, of course, also his reported pathological jealousy of, and reluctance to share with other Services – and double-cross deception can only be done with some form of a Twenty Committee bringing complete co-operation of all Services. The messages that were sent for Tricycle continued to be low-grade, trumpery stuff that any almost half-witted agent could have got. Even when a radio-transmitter was to be delivered to Tricycle, Hoover had to be persuaded with great difficulty not just to arrest the man who brought it. Then the F.B.I. sent radio reports on the transmitter, still low-grade, but – and it is almost impossible to believe – they never let Tricycle know what they had sent or what the Germans had asked. At last the Twenty Committee persuaded Hoover to let us have Tricycle back.

Colonel Robertson put the problem to Tricycle – he could end his double agent work with our gratitude or he could come back via Lisbon and try to explain away his failure in America and re-habilitate himself with his Abwehr masters. Tar Robertson warned him that his chances were nothing like even money. How was he to explain his complete failure in America in spite of having spent the large sum that they had given him? Even more difficult – how to explain his complete failure to do any of the things that he had been told to do? Worst of all, how to cover up his complete ignorance of anything that *he* had sent on the radio? The odds must be at least two to one that he was blown. And, if he was, it was pretty certain that he would be tortured to squeeze him dry of information about our system, and then there was equally probable death awaiting him at the end.

But Dusko Popov was determined to fight Hitler and the Nazis in the best way he could, and he went to Lisbon where, with his wonderful flair, he beat the odds and got away with it. It remains for me the greatest instance of cold-blooded courage that I have ever been in contact with.

To return to my own mission. After leaving Tricycle I had a wonderful day in New York with both children – because it was by now their holiday time and Howard Goodhart had invited them down to New York to join Iris and me. Next day I was due to leave for Halifax and home when a surprise message arrived from Washington. My orders were cancelled – the entry of America into the war had caused an urgent need to strengthen our naval intelligence mission and I was to return to Washington until extra officers could be got out from England.

So back we went, Iris and I. The Murdochs could not have us again as their family were coming to them for Christmas – but we managed to get a room at the Wardman Park Hotel. Then there arose the problem of money. The allowance that I had brought out with me had, naturally, been almost spent in anticipation of my return to England. The paymaster of H.M.S. *Saker* (the ship's name for our mission in Washington) refused to pay me anything as I was not 'on his books' and he had not even been notified of my arrival or orders to stay. Nothing would move him. I borrowed what I could from our Security Co-ordination but Iris and I had to feed solely in drug stores. Then Churchill came out to visit Roosevelt and, promptly, every crackpot in America wrote to him – 'I knew your mother, she was a lovely woman . . .', 'If you want to win the war, this is how to do it . . .' and so on. There were piles of letters in a room at the British Embassy and all had to be answered. They needed typists and I managed to get Iris taken on. One of the secretaries of the embassy (Tony, later Sir Anthony, Rumbold) devised a series of standard answers, marked each letter with the appropriate number – except for a few that needed individual answers – and Iris and others typed the indicated reply from 10 a.m. to 3 p.m., for thirty-three dollars a week. On her first pay-day we went out for a proper dinner!

The embassy made a mistake with their procedure over these letters. They threw the envelopes in which the letters had come into the 'trash bins'. They learned too late that the envelopes, addressed for the first time ever to a 'reigning' British Prime Minister at the White House itself, had become collectors' items and the janitor had been selling them off at prices which would have reduced our growing war debt.

It was wonderful to be with Iris, even if still separated from the children, and it was interesting to see how efficiently U.S. Naval Intelligence tabulated its information with the most modern office equipment and a prodigal use of manpower that we couldn't afford. But otherwise my work was routine. One day, at a meeting with Sir William Stephenson, he asked me if I would transfer to his staff, with a possibility of working Tricycle and conceivably other double agents, dealing with such Special Intelligence as they got and so on. If so, he would ask Uncle John to release me.

It was tempting. It sounded quite attractive as life in America was 'easier' than England in war-time and, best of all, I would be with the family. But I could not help longing to get back to my fascinating job in 17M in the real centre of things where I felt that I might contribute something really worthwhile, so I refused. But I came back at 'Little Bill'. I suggested that he should take Iris on. She could type and was efficient, and it seemed a more interesting and worthwhile job for her than the cloakroom at the Puritan Hotel. Little Bill expressed sorrow at my refusal, but agreed to the suggestion about Iris. From then on she was cleared for Special Intelligence and double cross and I could tell her what I was doing in 17M.

On 3 February 1942 I had an interesting experience. The U.S. Coastguard Service – which differs from ours in being a branch of their active sea-going service – held a large ceremony in a vast hall to swear in several hundred war-time officers, and our Naval Mission was asked for a suitable officer to address them on what

British yachtsmen were doing in the war. I was the only ex-yachtsman there, so I was detailed.

The ceremony was impressive, if theatrical. Then I gave a talk, and afterwards a group pressed round me with questions when the parade was dismissed. One said to me, 'I never knew before that the English had a sense of humour.' Then a newly sworn officer came up and said, 'You're the man, aren't you, who shaves with an electric razor going round the Fastnet.' I always used an electric razor and took it and a battery when sailing – I hate a scruffy beard and ordinary shaving is impossible in a yacht in a sea-way – but I couldn't conceive how he knew. He explained that Alf Loomis, the well-known American yachting journalist, used to lecture on the Fastnet race and his film showed me shaving with the Fastnet Rock in the background and I remembered how Alf, who had been navigator in Mike Mason's lovely *Latifa* in that race, had got me to pose for fun in *Latifa's* cockpit.

At last my replacement arrived and on 16 February we went to New York and next day I left for Halifax, there to board an armed merchant cruiser for the trip home to Glasgow. In the Clyde the Customs came on board and assembled us in the ship's saloon. Then their leader told us to fill up the forms distributed to us and warned us to be honest as they would check every fifth lot of luggage. He then gave good advice. 'As you've all probably got nylon stockings' (they were rare then) 'for your wives or girl-friends let me tell you that the duty on nylon is less than on silk – and the duty on cotton is highest of all – so don't make the mistake that the last lot I checked did.' The Customs Officer who went through my bags found three tins of pipe tobacco, looked at my list and found 'three pounds of tobacco' on it. As I had been honest in my list he said, 'Those aren't pound tins – bloody swindlers, these Yanks,' and altered the list to 'three-quarters of a pound – no duty.' I've always found the Customs to be human, if you're square with them.

In late February I reported back to Uncle John at the Admiralty, only to find that our relationship had reached its nadir. He was more offensive than I had ever known him to be – he gave me his frequent 'I'm only a simple sailor' gambit (sailor, yes – simple, never) and added in a blitz about 'just because you are a brilliant lawyer and much cleverer than I am, don't think you can wangle round *me*.' I could only think that the diatribe was caused by my being with Iris for seven weeks more than the deadline he had laid down, but *I* didn't bomb Pearl Harbor or send myself the order to stay. It was only later that I learnt from Commander Pearse, his secretary, that Little Bill had ignored my refusal to stay in the States and written to Uncle John asking for my transfer. I don't think that Uncle John ever accepted that I had not been behind the proposal.

8

Section 17M and the German Abwehr

The intercepted and deciphered messages, the Special Intelligence Ultra messages, that came into the Admiralty can be divided into three broad categories. First, the messages that might require naval operational action, mainly signals between German ships and between them and the German Naval H.Q. These went direct by teleprinter to the O.I.C.*

All the remainder came to Section 17M, usually by special despatch rider, though very urgent ones would be passed on the scrambler telephone. These formed the two other broad categories, the mass of messages of the Abwehr and deciphered messages from all other sources.

Our link with the O.I.C. was of great importance. The O.I.C.'s naval signals were dealt with by several sub-sections of Section 8, as it was numbered. Firstly there were the movements of surface ships. With regard to surface warships one can instance signals indicating that they were or were not preparing for sea, or going to sea and on what operation; when they were moving up or down the occupied coasts, especially the Norwegian coast in relation to the P.Q. (Russian) convoys and so on. Then there were messages about supply ships for U-boats, about surface raiders and their supply ships, special cargoes being brought from Japan, and many other categories. And then there were the vitally im-

* While this book was in the press the definitive history of the O.I.C. appeared in *Very Special Intelligence* by Patrick Beesley (Hamish Hamilton).

portant U-boat signals, the U-boat traffic as we called it, which
was dealt with by Section 8s.

In Section 8s the U-boat plot on the chart in the U-boat room
would show exactly where, within a quite small area, every U-boat
was, and Rodger Winn developed an almost incredible flair for
discerning what lay behind the signals. He could divine, usually
correctly and well in advance, what a particular U-boat or U-boat
packs were likely to do, whether they were moving to a new
hunting area or returning home and so on, and the signals would
often reveal the U-boat's fuel or torpedo reserves. The knowledge
gained from these signals, coupled with that flair of Rodger
Winn's, backed as he was by an excellent Section, enabled him to
say with an astonishing degree of accuracy where U-boats would
be tomorrow from positions given two days ago when the signal
was transmitted. This was the foundation for the 'evasive routing'
and changes of course en route given to convoys, thus saving much
shipping and many lives. These predictions were also the foundation for a close liaison with C-in-C Western Approaches so that he
could organize and vector hunting groups of corvettes and frigates
to the right areas of the Atlantic and Bay of Biscay. The
Admiralty could do the same with escorts or warships on passage
which were operated by them.

These successes were obtained without the Germans ever realizing their cause, a fact which was mainly due to the skill with
which our operations were ordered and carried out, but was also
helped by the Germans deceiving themselves as to the cause of the
U-boats' diminishing successes and casualties, a misconception
which our double agents were able to encourage.

Although 17M had no part in the operational work or responsibilities of the O.I.C., it was part of our job to visit them at least
once a day so that we could try to help them if any of our traffic
threw a background light on theirs or if any of our traffic needed
operational action, and so that we could know what was going
on to help us to do our own job.

A minor instance of that liaison occurred in 1941. The German
agents in the United States were, as we have seen, a poor lot, and
few had radio sets. One of their jobs was to report the sailings of
ships for any British destination, in the U.K. or abroad, and of

any convoys. As these messages were conveyed by letter via Lisbon, the Abwehr there sent their contents on by radio to Germany. These arrived too late for any operational use and were probably only useful for information on our economy, the Germans being helped for operational purposes for a time by *their* deciphering of our messages in a particular cipher about convoys to and from Halifax. Nevertheless, the traffic did help the O.I.C. with background as to what the Germans knew about the positions of our ships and the pattern of sailings.

In 1942 we accumulated enough evidence against the Spanish trawler *Primer Enrique* and even more against the *Segundo Enrique* to justify their being stopped and taken in to Gibraltar; after questioning, based ostensibly on other sources, the two skippers and two W/T operators were imprisoned in the U.K., which reduced the popularity among other skippers of this form of spying. Also in 1942 we got an interesting series of signals from the Abwehr in Spain about an undertaking in Vigo. These eventually established that the skipper and W/T operator of the Icelandic trawler *Arctic* had been suborned while in that port. After consultation with the O.I.C. the First Sea Lord decided that the *Arctic's* fishing area would make her reports potentially dangerous and that she should be stopped. It was therefore arranged to pull her in, and also to pull in another quite innocent trawler to protect our sources. *Arctic's* skipper and W/T operator confessed and were detained – the trawler being released after most helpful undertakings from the Icelandic government. Our authorities were faced with a problem over the other trawler. She had been arrested by an American ship, which was in the appropriate area and the most convenient one to use, and we were given a confession from her skipper and W/T operator. However our authorities quickly learnt that there was serving in the American ship a tough ex-New York cop who had put them through a fierce interrogation. Their complete innocence was speedily established and they and their trawler were immediately released. So much for third degree!

Another example out of many instances of direct co-operation between 17M and the O.I.C. was due to fortunate timing of events outside our control. During one of the brief periods when the O.I.C. was not receiving U-boat signals almost as speedily as the Germans themselves, the Germans were inept enough twice to notify the Abwehr at Lisbon of impending U-boat concentrations, and on two other occasions of intensified air attacks, all on convoys to the peninsula.

A final example of that fruitful co-operation with the O.I.C. may be recorded here although the Special Intelligence came from a different source and not from the Abwehr. We were reading the radio messages sent between the German Armistice Commission in Toulon and Berlin. These messages gave us absolutely accurate information about intended movements of warships of the French Navy, including details of the purpose of any movement, for instance exercises or manoeuvres, and also destination details of ships leaving port. Sometimes the messages were received by us some days in advance of the movement. They were of assistance to the O.I.C. and, if the ships were going to make a passage, they should have been of value to operational commands. These messages also helped the French Section of N.I.D. when they reported that ships were going for an exercise thereby enabling the French Section to dismiss as inaccurate reports which they got from time to time from our Secret Service agents in the South of France that the French Navy was going to start an operation or be transferred abroad.

Another German activity in the peninsula caused us anxiety and gave us an exercise in detection which led to a considerable success. In December 1941 and January 1942 a merchant ship and a small warship blew up from an unknown cause while anchored off Gibraltar.

On 29 July 1942 we got a message which had been sent from Madrid to Berlin two days before. It read when translated:

476. To ERBE. For ZWILLING. Ref. your Most Secret 11/16/42 of 20/7. Car X no. 2154 repair on 19/7 in Sesera. 3 part monobloc engine with 30 kgs. of fuel. Sparking-plug type 75 and 3 valves 38E with eating away on 4/8. Attachment on left centre seat left. Sparking-plug has failed. Car now in Basta. Is under observation.

HUMBERTO KOSP

We knew from previous messages that Erbe was the head of the Spanish Section of the Abwehr in Berlin, that Zwilling was the Abwehr sabotage H.Q. in Berlin, that Humberto KOSP was the sabotage group at Abwehr Station in Madrid, that Sesera was Seville and Basta was Gibraltar. The elucidation of the message would still have been difficult though we might have managed with shipping lists, etc., but we got unexpected help from the Germans. They sent another signal on the same day which read:

'Ref. message 476. X equals IMBER.

We therefore interpreted the original message to read:

476. For the head of Spanish Section in Berlin. For Sabotage H.Q. Berlin. Ref. your Most Secret (letter) 11/16/42 of 20/7. Ship *Imber* ship no. 2154 was sabotaged on 19/7 in Seville. A bomb with 3 parts with 30 kilogrammes of explosive (was used). Fuse type 75 and 3 slow action fuses set to go off on 4th August. Attachment to left centre seat left (we failed to interpret this). Immediate action fuse has failed. Ship now in Gibraltar. Is under observation.

Sabotage Section Madrid

Urgent instructions were sent to FOCNA (Flag Officer in Command, North Atlantic) at Gibraltar, and divers discovered that German skin-divers in Seville had fixed a new and most interesting type of limpet mine to the port side of the port bilge keel of the SS *Imber*, nearly amidships, giving the interpretation of the phrase that had defeated us. With the good fortune that the immediate action fuse failed, this message saved the *Imber* and gave us the interesting limpet mine.

The Germans had no further successes with limpet mining as we were able to take precautions without compromising our source. Indeed the Germans even helped us to defeat what they described as a most promising operation with active Spanish help in favourable conditions in Las Palmas by informing us in advance of its date and details.

The Italians, on the other hand, had four successes in Gibraltar. But then we were not reading their messages!

The ship-reporting service in the Gibraltar area was of great value to the Germans. It was obvious and inevitable that the Germans would know about any ship which arrived at Gibraltar as the dockyard was full of Spanish workmen who crossed the border each day. That had to be accepted. But far more serious was the fact that the Germans set up radio reporting stations along the shores on both sides of the Straits of Gibraltar and, later, on Alboran Island. These gained in efficiency and, after a while, no warship could even *pass* unreported in good visibility. In daylight names and details would be included in the messages.

That great sailor and great character, Admiral Somerville, had done his best while in command at Gibraltar to fool the Germans by starting off in one direction and turning back when out at sea and other means. On some occasions, when he was not on board, his flagship 'wore his flag' and on some occasions did not do so when he was in command. The intention of course was to confuse German reports – if he was not on board an operation of any magnitude was improbable. Interestingly enough, another Admiral refused to use this subterfuge. 'Nelson always flew his flag – so will I' was his attitude.

But such subterfuges were not enough. The Germans enjoyed the whole-hearted co-operation of Franco's fascist officers and ministers. Besides the stations I have mentioned, the Germans got their information from Spanish service stations of various kinds, lighthouse keepers and some Spanish naval vessels. On one occasion, when the Germans thought that a convoy might have slipped through in bad visibility one night, they got the Spaniards to lay on a special air reconnaissance flight for their benefit.

It was impossible to do anything to stop this flow of intelligence to Germany without running an unacceptable risk of compromising our sources. All that could be done was to try to arrange that ships should pass through the Straits at times and in conditions least helpful to the Germans. This was, on some occasions, successfully done and based on our Special Intelligence.

But then came an even more dangerous development. The Germans spent six months, and much money, in setting up scientific spotting stations in specially erected buildings on specially prepared sites along the Straits. These had very elaborate equipment based on something that they called a bolometer which worked, in so far as I could understand it, by infra-red rays, and had sufficient accuracy to detect the size of any ship passing by measuring the heat of her funnels. Their range extended clear across the Straits and they would be unaffected by weather conditions.

The question was how this could be stopped without blowing Special Intelligence. 17M had got the positions of these sites pretty accurately from the messages. Aerial photos from out at sea were taken at intervals and, in conjunction with our data on the rate of progress in construction, the actual buildings were pinpointed exactly by the excellent R.A.F. photo-interpreting unit in spite of camouflage of the buildings and masts for reception, and so on.

The danger was taken so seriously by the Operations Staff that even a commando raid was discussed, but this was eventually vetoed because of the diplomatic and international dangers. We managed to supply the Foreign Office with enough information for them to persuade our ever-reluctant Ambassador to protest to the Spanish Government. After long delay the Spanish Government acted.

We were glad to note from the Special Intelligence traffic that they acted before, though only just before, the stations were ready to operate. We were less glad to learn that the action had followed long enough after a warning to the Germans for them to have time to remove their equipment. The Spaniards duly reported to our ambassador that they had raided the places indicated but they were merely sea-side villas, innocent of any equipment such as we had alleged to be in them. We were interested to learn from the traffic that the cost to the Germans of this frustrated enterprise was great and had been increased by the cost of two Mercedes cars given as a reward to the Spaniards most concerned in providing the required delay. Incidentally, the steady increase in my knowledge of the Spanish readiness to lie to us *officially* was of great use in the later planning of Operation Mincemeat, *The Man Who Never Was.*

Another ticklish series of operations by us concerned the frustration of German attempts to smuggle through our blockade. I say 'ticklish' because our problem was, as ever, how to take action without compromising our sources. The Germans were increasingly short of a number of vital materials, and particularly of platinum, necessary for much of their electronic equipment, and industrial diamonds. So they built up an ever growing smuggling operation from South America through the Peninsula. We, of course, got our knowledge from our regular informants, the Abwehr in Madrid and Lisbon. When the messages between them and Berlin, and *vice versa*, only indicated the supplier of a consignment all we could do was to warn the Director of the Economic Warfare Division (D.E.W.D.), without revealing our source. This caused us no difficulty as he was prepared to act on a highly graded report, usually B1 on the grading system, and our information *could* easily have come from a British spy in the country concerned. This method was safe as long as we were careful not to link timing too closely with the relevant radio messages – but, equally, there was not often much that D.E.W.D. could do other than black-listing and so on.

More interesting were the occasions when the smuggler and the ship were identified – but even then the indication quite often was not more precise than 'a steward on the S.S. So and So'. However the Navy was frequently able to board the ship and conduct a search detailed enough to find the diamonds or platinum – especially if those conducting the search were provided with two or three names, including the right one. This system, coupled with the stopping and searching of some non-suspect ships, succeeded in avoiding compromising our source, and in the recovery of much contraband. In fact 17M considered offering to surrender our pay for a commission on the value of the diamonds and platinum recovered!

We learned also that the Germans prepared Intelligence Commandos (Abwehr-Truppen) who would go with any troops that spearheaded an invasion. These would go direct to any headquarters, ministry or other important place or office in any invaded town in order to preserve and collect any codes, ciphers, plans, records or other documents before they became scattered or destroyed. This knowledge not only gave D.N.I. the idea of forming similiar naval intelligence commandos when we, in our turn, went on to the offensive but, most importantly, the contents of the German signals about their formation and training gave us the first indication of a possible German operation.

From such signals we got advance information that the Germans were planning invasions of Yugoslavia, Greece, Crete and the Caucasus. I say 'planning', because the Germans, like us, often planned operations which were either postponed for some time or abandoned altogether. Even this did not matter as they took care to send messages indicating that there was to be delay, that the operation was abandoned, or that it was now imminent. Their Abwehr-Truppen were especially successful in the Balkans, under a man named Obladen. They kept up with the front-line troops, linked with fifth-columnists and agents, guided, directed and reported and, at times, had the only W/T sets operating in the front line so that the military had to use them. The speed and accuracy of their reports was most impressive, especially in Athens and Greek ports, and they gave their H.Q. (and us) much valuable information.

From time to time the Abwehr traffic would reveal the Germans' intention to try to work a deception on us. They had not the facilities that we had with our double-cross agents, and their operations of this kind were usually pretty low-level and inept, for instance planting lots of stories on unsuspecting merchant seamen. Sometimes it was done on a higher level, using 'neutral' diplomats, usually the Spanish of course. Occasionally these higher level attempts were more dangerous. A neutral diplomat, known to be pro-British, would have planted on him a story about an important development and he, in complete innocence, would pass it on 'as a service to us'. Or some similiar information could be planted on one of our diplomats or other visitors abroad. To be forearmed was a great benefit.

The Abwehr in Norway provided us with an interesting check in the reverse direction. Before one of the North Russian PQ convoys Admiral Sir John Tovey, when he was C.-in-C., Home Fleet, had the idea that, if he made a feint with the supporting heavy ships towards Norway before steaming north, it might cause the Germans to think that there was going to be an attack on that country, or at least a bombardment of some ports or installations, and so draw away some of the U-boats, ships and aircraft which might attack the convoy. In the result, this manoeuvre did not seem to have had that result, but the Abwehr wireless traffic from Norway showed that there had been an alert and 'stand to' along the relevant parts of the Norwegian coast at the appropriate time, and there did not seem to be any other cause for this having happened.

Finally, there were signals from that Abwehr station, from time to time, which revealed that they were going to conduct security sweeps in particular coastal areas, or sometimes an army exercise. These might be dangerous as S.O.E. (the Special Operations Executive who operated saboteurs, etc., in Europe) sometimes landed their agents on that coast and the two events might coincide.

'C' had, quite reasonably, made it a strict rule that we might not pass any Special Intelligence information, however well camouflaged, to anyone outside the Navy – and he strongly suspected, again quite reasonably in the light of experience, that the security of S.O.E. was not too good. However, D.N.I. noticed that the liason between the appropriate one of 'C' 's officers and the 'named officer' in S.O.E. to whom some Special Intelligence information was passed was not too efficient – it is not for me to indicate which of the two was to blame for this. D.N.I. therefore ordered me to warn the particular S.O.E. officer if 17M noticed any indication of danger of this kind.

At a meeting of the Joint Intelligence Committee the Head of S.O.E. said to D.N.I., 'Thank heaven that your people let me know that the Germans were going to be active yesterday or some of my people would have run into real trouble. I just managed to call it off in time.' 'C' overheard this, became suspicious and investigated. The warning could only have emanated from Special Intelligence.

I was sent for by Uncle John who showed me a letter from 'C'. This said that he had discovered that Lieutenant-Commander Montagu had been passing information based on Special Intelligence direct to S.O.E. This was contrary to the agreement with D.N.I. and unless it was stopped immediately, no further

Special Intelligence would be passed to the Admiralty while it went to Lieutenant-Commander Montagu.

D.N.I. showed me his reply. Lieutenant-Commander Montagu had been severely reprimanded and this practice would stop forthwith. He then smiled, and said: 'It would be wrong to risk loss of life by delaying warning S.O.E. There'll only be a long dispute if I argue it out with 'C' – so I'm sending that letter, but you are to carry on as before.'

As usual, Uncle John was right. But I did ask for his order to be put in writing, to be kept in 17M's safe, in case he was hit by a bomb or run over by a bus. To my surprise, he agreed.

9

The Orange Summaries

The Abwehr signal traffic was not even the major part of the Special Intelligence work of 17M. Our directive was broadly phrased as 'the control and handling of all Special Intelligence which did not concern movements of enemy ships', and there was a mass of other Special Intelligence covering every other aspect apart from the purely naval one.

Between December 1940, when Joan Saunders and I started, and the end of 1941, the signals that came into the section for us to deal with increased from between 25 and 30 a day, mainly Abwehr, right up to a figure which fluctuated between 200 and 300. From then on the flow continued its upward trend, not, of course, as steeply as earlier and with fluctuations when one or other of the ciphers used had been changed and therefore had to be re-broken.

Indeed there was one occasion of near disaster. The O.S.S. (the Office of Strategic Services, roughly the American equivalent of our S.O.E.) burgled the office of the Japanese Military Attaché in Portugal and there managed to get a quite high-level diplomatic cipher. They had warned no one of their intention and did not know that we and the Americans had broken that cipher and were reading the messages sent in it. Had the Japanese realized what had happened and changed the cipher, it would have meant at least a long break in our reading messages in the new one. A huge risk for no gain! Similarly we had to keep the capture of a German U-Boat secret for several reasons, the most

important being that, if the Germans had learned of the capture
and had been worried whether the Captain had destroyed his
cipher machine and materials in time, and had changed their
cipher as a precaution, we would have had a disastrous break
in reading the vital U-Boat traffic.

The steady overall increase came from a multitude of derivations, apart from occasional sources which also could be of high
level and great importance. These derivations can be broadly
defined as German military signals, which included both army
and air force messages, German and other diplomatic signals,
especially one of the Japanese diplomatic ciphers – and the German Armistice Commission with the French. I should add that
the German army and airforce signals ranged from the movements, strengths, supplies, etc., and the plans of units of all sizes,
up through similar information from Rommel and commanders
in Russia, Italy and elsewhere to the German High Command
and Hitler himself, to complete discussions on tactics and strategy
as well as vitally important 'Fuehrer Commands', commands
which could not be disobeyed. Instances of these last were such
orders as the 'no withdrawal' sent to Stalingrad with its fatal
results and also similar orders from time to time after D-day in
France. For example these included such orders as the forbid-
ding of a planned withdrawal of (say) a tank brigade which a
commander in the field had notified would become necessary.

The Japanese diplomatic messages often included long conversations between the ambassador or his senior staff and Hitler
or his ministers, recounting how Hitler saw the war, German
economy and weapon manufacture and so on, as well as long-
term strategic plans. The Sicherheitsdienst (Himmler's State
Security Service, the S.D.) representative at Vichy, Dr Richter,
was a close personal friend of Laval's and his messages to Berlin
revealed much of great importance.

A problem for D.N.I. was how to distribute this information
and to whom. Distribution was strictly limited on a *realistic* 'need
to know' principle. Even then the absolutely vital need to safeguard the fact that we were cipher-breaking necessitated a 'sheep
and goats' division. The very few who had to know the exact words
that had been received – and to know it without delay – got that as

D

'Top Secret–U', Ultra Secret information under special precautions. The remainder got the information carefully paraphrased and camouflaged but with the A1 grading which was sparingly used. This system worked efficiently and we remained confident that there were no leaks.

The few who were to get the Special Intelligence 'straight', in its original form, were limited to the First Lord, the First Sea Lord, also known as the Chief of Naval Staff, and a very select few of his principal operational staff – the Vice-Chief of Naval Staff, the two Assistant Chiefs of Naval Staff, Home and Foreign, and the similar two Directors of the two Operational Divisions and the Director of Plans. These obviously needed the information for background to strategic planning.

Efficient distribution to those few within the Admiralty who had the messages 'straight' was difficult to devise. At first, when the messages were few, it could be done by hand, but it was clear that that could not last. Soon we were distributing 'summaries' on special orange-coloured paper which was used for nothing else. These summaries were placed in specially made boxes with Bramah locks and were taken by special messengers to the recipients, each of whom had a key. These recipients could be trusted not to put the summaries anywhere except in the box, and the boxes were collected when the next summary was delivered, and brought back to us so that we could check the safe return of the documents.

17M put out two editions a day, morning and evening, and occasional special issues if something of great or urgent importance came through.

The contents consisted of the messages or the relevant or important parts of them. In accordance with D.N.I.'s excellent basic rule, these were unaltered and nothing additional might be inserted by way of explanation or evaluation. After the message ended we could, and usually had to, add the word 'Comment' and then add our comments. This was an important and difficult part of our work. These comments ranged from such as 'This makes a total of 30,000 men and 5,000 tanks at such and such a place' to 'Other messages on such and such dates show that Laval does not trust Monsieur X and is unlikely to act on this advice'. As the previous Orange Summaries had been collected by us a reply by Hitler to a request by Rommel would have to be followed by a 'Comment' setting out a summary of any necessary points from the earlier messages. If any additional information was needed by the recipient, we were rung on the scrambler phone or sent for. Such examples will suffice to show that much had to be done, at high pressure, to get the summaries out, completely up-to-the-minute and without delay. The First Sea Lord, for instance, regarded it as essential that he should have read his copy of the morning summary before going to the Chiefs of Staff meeting, and there was a hell of a row if it was delayed!

To cope with this there had to be a basic division of work, but this was kept flexible. Joan Saunders and Marjorie Boxall dealt with Abwehr, Pauline Fenley and Pat Trehearne were the experts on the German armed forces and kept their 'order of battle', while Robin Bartlett and the two last of those 'edited' the summaries on a rota basis. The sublieutenants, and later the Wren officers, were watchkeepers, the one who was on duty during day-time helped generally but the one who was on at night prepared the items for inclusion in the 'morning edition' for the duty editor's final approval, if necessary after reference to me. Our magnificent typists then rushed the result into type, banging out enough 'tops and carbons' on the dreadful Admiralty-issue typewriters – how they did it, and did it so quickly and accurately, was a miracle. They and the other girls also helped to work the various filing systems and had to have the great ability and memory to cope with the complete indexing that was necessary.

As newspapers are prone to boast how they got an issue printed and distributed without delay in spite of some serious dislocation, I must just claim an equivalent feat for the editorial staff of the Orange Summaries. One night the duty sub-lieutenant had to open a drawer of one of the filing cabinets. Inside was a cat giving birth to kittens. Keeping his head, he extracted the right file without disturbing the process. For the rest of the night, each time he opened the drawer, there was another kitten. By morning the cat had produced six kittens, and 17M had produced the Orange Summary in time to reach the First Sea Lord before he had to go to the Chiefs of Staff meeting.

We got a huge series of messages dealing with convoys carrying urgently needed petrol, ammunition, etc., across the Mediterranean to Rommel. These were included in the Orange Summaries because of their background value on whether Rommel could or could not carry out his plans, but they were dealt with operationally simultaneously by the O.I.C. These enabled us to sink a larger proportion of these supplies than we could otherwise have done, and thus cripple Rommel's army. Incidentally, much praise is due to those who so managed our operations that they drained Rommel of supplies without compromising our sources of information – no naval sweep, no submarine patrol and no bombing flight was ordered to be at the right spot at the right time to intercept. Either one of several air reconnaissances sent to different areas – including, of course, the right one – sighted the German-Italian convoy first or seaborne sweeps were ordered which would 'just happen' to reach the right spot at the right time, a neat piece of navigational planning!

It was also interesting to watch the parallel developments in the way these messages were used in the land fighting. General Montgomery, who commanded the 8th Army in the desert at that time, was clearly a great leader who really inspired confidence in his troops, but we could not help feeling, as we watched action following 'intelligence', that it was somewhat easier to defeat your opponent if you knew in advance just where his troops, tanks and other defences were, how many in each place, how short he was of petrol or ammunition and exactly what his plans were, both if he (the opponent) was successful but also if he wasn't. Montgomery had this advantage in North Africa, and, incidentally, he and Eisenhower had it to nearly the same extent in Normandy. In the later campaign from just before the German counter-offensive in the Ardennes much of the signal traffic went by land line and so was unavailable.

It was also necessary to include the Hitler–Rommel military and planning signals in the Orange Summaries, and this illustrates well the purpose of the summaries. Such information was obviously necessary for the naval top-brass who had to plan ahead and needed to forecast how the war in North Africa would develop and bring changing naval responsibilities and

requirements. But there was even more to it than that. The First
Sea Lord needed to know everything that was available if he was
to pull his full weight and use his great abilities in the discussion
at Chiefs of Staff Committee meetings.

It is greatly to the credit of John Godfrey, who saw that these
needs would exist if Special Intelligence developed as it in
fact did, and devised the Orange Summary system to meet them,
that it turned out so successful. A mark of that fact was shown
when the Chief of Air Staff kept finding that the First Sea Lord
knew something important at a meeting and he hadn't got the
information yet, or if a bit of information was discussed and the
First Sea Lord already could see how it tied in with something
else from our 'comments'. The C.A.S. demanded the same service
from Air Intelligence and a most able officer came to 17M to see
how we did it. He was already a Wing-Commander and we were
interested to see, when he returned for a chat and with some
queries, just after he had inaugurated a similar system in the Air
Ministry, that he had risen to Group-Captain. Of course there
may well have been other reasons but it didn't please members
of our team, who remained static in rank throughout the war.
The usual acid comments about relative ranks in the Navy and
R.A.F. arose again!

But the subjects on which we got intelligence were so numerous
that it will help to list some of them:

1. Advance warnings, becoming more and more definite, of
    the German intention to invade Russia.
2. A very considerable amount of information about German
    plans and the progress of the war in Russia. Much of this
    came from the Japanese diplomatic messages.
3. German intentions to invade the Balkans and their difficul-
    ties there. This last became very important.
4. German diplomatic relations with other countries, their
    démarches and negotiations.
5. German 'appreciations' of what *our* intentions might be and
    their plans to counter them.
6. German measures and defences against our invasion of
    France and plans for counter attack if we landed. Later

there was proof of the developing success of our 'cover operations'.

7. German plans and movements of troops from one front to another.
8. Information about the gradual internal disintegration of Germany and its economy.
9. The attempted assassination of Hitler* in July 1944 – and eventually his transfer of power to his successor.
10. German peace *démarches* before the end.
11. German intentions to use new weapons and varyingly detailed descriptions of the weapons and their potentialities – including our *first* knowledge of V.1 and V.2, and of human torpedoes, rocket bombs, new type U-boats, new type torpedoes and so on. Again, some of this came through the Japanese diplomatic traffic.
12. Relations between the Germans and Japanese, including attempts by the Japanese to get U-boats sent to the Far East for active service as well as the occasions when U-boats were to be used for transport in both directions, particularly when German radar was sent to the Japanese whose own radar was then very poor indeed.

I will develop three of these categories more fully.

First, the war in the Balkans. Quite early on we could see clearly, from this constant stream, and it gradually became more and more definite, that the only force that was really *fighting* steadily and consistently against the Germans was Tito's partisans. General Mihailovic's Chetniks began to co-operate more and more with the Germans and to fight actively together with them against Tito. We got more and more information about the planning and execution of this internecine warfare which greatly assisted the Germans. Its culmination, in one sense, was when we received the Abwehr report of how one of Mihailovic's most senior officers had been awarded an *Allied* decoration for his services – and how the *Germans* threw a good party in their

---

* It was, perhaps, our biggest thrill of the war when we got the premature messages, sent out by the conspirators, saying that Hitler was dead. And the biggest let-down when we got the official and correct version.

officers' mess to celebrate it with him! The more important of these messages were, of course, included in the Orange Summaries. Whether they had any effect on our policy or not, I don't know, though the First Sea Lord expressed great interest in this development. In any case it was impressive to note the change in the tone of these intercepted messages, and the increase in the German difficulties, as we transferred our support to Tito.

Secondly, from the run-up to Operation Overlord, through the D-day landings, right up to the German counter-offensive in the Ardennes in December 1944, we got an absorbingly interesting flow of messages which were of vital importance, both to the strategic planners and to the commanders in the field.

As the build-up developed the messages revealed three things in particular. Hitler, the German High Command and their generals in the field were all accepting the deception put over by double agents that our build-up was directed against the Pas de Calais. Also their lack of information from sources other than those controlled by us had prevented their realizing that we were building huge artificial harbours (the Mulberries), so that they considered that we would try to invade through ports and not over open beaches as we in fact did. Finally, we learnt that they feared landings at high tide rather than at low tide.

As we landed we learnt that the Germans were not moving up their reserves because they were still convinced that the landings in Normandy were merely a strong diversionary attack as a prelude to the main invasion in the Pas de Calais.

Then, right through the campaign, we learnt of every plan, except, of course, those organized by landline, that Hitler or the High Command made with their generals. The latter reported, and asked leave to move tanks and troops and we learnt what was authorized and what was turned down. As a result, to cite one example, Montgomery's steady battle to break out from the beach-head against most of the German tanks was continued until, at last, the Germans, who had still been refused help from the strategic reserve because of our threat to the Pas de Calais, moved more of their remaining tanks from another sector in Normandy to face him – and then, and only then, General Bradley made his break-out.

And so it continued as the campaign developed. One of the high spots was when Eisenhower was able to surround much of the German armies after Special Intelligence had warned him of the detailed planning of the big major counter-attack by the Germans.

Not the least interesting and important of the intercepted messages were the personal interventions of Hitler himself. As the Allies gained successes so Hitler's distrust of the ability of his generals increased – and his personal ukases, the Fuehrer orders which *had* to be obeyed to the letter, became more and more frequent. It was always exciting, indeed encouraging, when we read a decree (like the ones that lost the German army at Stalingrad) that there were to be *no* withdrawals, not a metre of ground was to be given up, in spite of the arguments by the generals that a tactical reforming of their lines was essential in order to avert disaster.

All this was both fascinating for us in 17M and, although *prima facie* not naval, was of great importance to the recipients of the Orange Summaries – not only the First Sea Lord and the Vice-Chief of Naval Staff in their Chief of Staff and Vice-Chief rôles with strategic planning responsibilities, but also to our other recipients in their forward planning to meet future naval commitments. For the commanders in the field it was, of course, vital to their eventual success.

Thirdly, the Japanese diplomatic traffic. The Germans were, throughout the war, anxious to impress the Japanese and to 'keep them sweet'. Long messages were sent back to Tokyo about how the war was going in Russia, difficulties experienced, plans for the future, both immediate and long-term. Full details of how the Germans felt the other campaigns, including the U-boat war, were going. Long details about weapon development, etc., discussions about the German economy, and about what Allied plans were thought to be, outright attempts to get the Japanese into the war. A multiplicity of subjects.

The German who was the informant, or the German participant in a discussion, could be anyone from, quite frequently, Hitler himself downwards, and similarly the Japanese could be anyone from the ambassador to a Service attaché.

This traffic, of course, presented a problem. The facts in the signals were by no means necessarily the truth, far from it. But it became noticeable that *some* German informants felt it best not to minimize their difficulties and dangers. *Some* felt that it was right to tell the Japanese the truth about weapons and so on. *Most* felt that it was right to tell them the truth about German plans. After all, before she came into the war, Japan was as near as makes no odds a non-fighting ally – and it seemed that the Germans were confident that the Japanese would 'keep their mouths shut'. But one always had to remember that the Germans were bound to try to keep the Japanese convinced that they would win the war, so there was a temptation for them to stress the bright side and minimize the dark. On the other hand it was also a good line for them to highlight their difficulties in order to show the wonderful way in which they overcame them.

With great speed we had to check, where possible, from other traffic and other intelligence sources to include our 'Comment'. In addition we had to gain experience of the line that a particular German usually took, frank or propagandist, and, where a Japanese transmitted a summary or a comment, whether he was gullible or astute, violently pro-German or realistic, and so on.

Uncle John, being Uncle John, realized that some item about, let us say, St Nazaire might seem to us too unimportant for inclusion if we did not know that a raid on that port was being considered. But it *would* then be important even if that plan had not yet got sufficiently definite for the appropriate N.I.D. Section to be asked for intelligence about it.

For that reason he took two steps to keep me informed. First, I was made the alternate Admiralty representative to Captain 'Ginger' Lewis on the Inter Service Security Board and when I did not attend the meetings Ginger Lewis kept me informed. This body met at least once a week. It had information about all plans at a very early stage, a factor that also linked closely with my double-cross deception work. This gave me assistance which my other Service colleagues on the Twenty Committee lacked.

The second measure was that Uncle John ensured that I as an individual was sent for to read any paper, however high-level or secret, that he might have – Chiefs of Staff minutes, memoranda, and so on – even some War Cabinet directives.

This was essential if the First Sea Lord, First Lord and so on were to get the service that they needed. But what could be more enthralling than to read both what our rulers were thinking and planning and also, simultaneously, what Hitler and the German High Command were thinking and planning?

There was yet another duty concerned with Special Intelligence. Each day 'C' himself, or sometimes one of his officers, took to the Prime Minister a document on the lines of our Orange Summary – without, I was interested to note, our useful 'Comments'. From time to time Winston would want to raise a query on, or make a suggestion arising out of, a naval matter recorded in the document. He then wrote in the margin, in red ink '1.S.L.' (for First Sea Lord'), added the question and his initials. Sometimes it was simply 'I.S.L. Why? W.S.C.' Sometimes the question would be longer and more precise and sometimes, if he felt that we might counter a German action or make use of a German belief or weakness, he would make a suggestion.

The document would then be put in a locked box and Lady Dunne (the wife of an old friend of mine, the Chief Metropolitan Magistrate) would tramp along the corridor in the FANY uniform of the Women's Transport Corps, and when we were ready with the answer, she would come back and fetch the box.

My job was to find out the answer, have it and a covering chit to be signed by D.N.I. typed out, take them to D.N.I. and then take them personally to the First Sea Lord, get him to sign the answer and then send it back to 'C' for the Prime Minister.

To get the answer was not always easy. It could mean pumping someone in the Admiralty who was not in the Special Intelligence picture, and if so it would need a lot of pretty skilful dissimulation! For a Lieutenant-Commander R.N.V.R. to ask why we did not (let us say) lay a whole lot of mines somewhere, or why we haven't got a weapon that can do so-and-so, without giving any reason other than 'D.N.I. needs to know', or in desperation, 'the First Sea Lord wants to know from D.N.I.', would either get no answer or it might well be 'if the First Sea Lord wants to know, I'll answer when I get a request in the normal way'. It was not only from my work in deceiving the Germans that I learnt the fascination of the 'criminal life' of fraud, false pretences and so on, as well as its difficulties and snags.

Another thing was interesting about these queries from the Prime Minister. Sometimes the writing was almost illegible and wandered down the side of the margin. On more than one occasion the covering note that I drafted, for D.N.I. to sign and submit to the First Sea Lord, read: 'The Prime Minister's question (or suggestion) appears to be' followed by the best guess or deciphering possible and then: 'If that is correct the following answer is submitted for your approval and signature.' The hand may have been unsteady for some reason, but his mind always remained brilliant and the questions or suggestions outstandingly acute.

All this, with the double-cross on which Norman Clackson helped me, constituted an enormous work-load and it could only be borne by the quality of the team, which was as industrious as it was happy. There was always something going on to keep up our spirits in spite of the arduous work and poor conditions. One neutral ambassador in London helped to keep us happy during a gloomy period of the war; he was obviously out to get a high decoration for valour and he cheered us every morning with a message to his home government consisting mainly of a lurid account of the number and nearness of the bombs that had fallen round his embassy and the courage with which he had extinguished fire-bombs. These messages were particularly entertaining as his embassy was within sight of my mother's house, so that I could report to the Section that no bomb of any kind had fallen within at least a couple of miles!

But the biggest factor was that, with very few exceptions, we were allowed to remain not only our own masters (largely because no one else understood our work – perhaps also as we were 'giving satisfaction') but also almost entirely without changes of personnel. This last was because Uncle John felt that our work was so secret that knowledge of it couldn't be spread, and also he realized that our experience of past messages and patterns of messages was invaluable.

10

The Twenty Committee Recruits its Double Agents

Out of some one hundred and twenty double agents who were operated for varying lengths of time – a few for only a day or two before failing to make real contact with the German spymasters (the German Abwehr officers controlling them), though many others for longer periods – the Twenty Committee operated some thirty-nine really effective double agents for substantial periods. As some of these built up networks of sub-agents, mostly fictitious, there were approximately the same number of sub-agents as well.

The members of the Twenty Committee carefully kept aloof from the agents, though exceptional circumstances might require a meeting, and I am therefore ignorant of the details of the fascinating art of operating them. It required an infinite measure of tact, patience, and hard work, as well as meticulous recording. This last was vital, though the reason may not at first be obvious. Section B.1A knew all the agents and knew what they had sent to the Germans, but by and large no two agents knew one another or what another agent had sent. It would have been all too easy to get wires crossed and for A to refer in a message to something that B had sent, or to base something in his attitude or his messages on something in C's past, his past either *before* or since he arrived in this country, but that, or any similar slip, could have been fatal. And the case officers had always to bear in mind the instructions of each agent as to where he was or was not to go and what he was to report on. One could not use X, who happened to be near an airfield to report (deceptively) about a bomb fitted to a particular type of fighter plane if he was a man who was stupid about machines, as some people are. Similarly, if one high-grade agent had been asked if a big munitions factory had been started at place X and policy had made us get him to report in the negative, and then a second high-grade agent was asked the same question some months later, the latter could not be allowed to report that there was a well established factory there even if policy had changed because bombing had stopped and the appropriate authorities wanted to exaggerate our manufacture of munitions. The second case officer would have to be alert enough to check what might have been reported before and the grade of the agent who had reported it. It would be all too easy to make a slip which would have been fatal to the credibility of at least one of the agents.

On top of all that, every agent quite naturally had his own 'style' in which he reported – these ranged from Tate, who always wrote even his letters as if he was composing a telegram, to Garbo, who always wrote in the flowery prose natural to a Spaniard. When a case officer was writing a report in the name of one of the many wholly imaginary agents or sub-agents it was not always easy to remember which one wrote in what style. And a mistake could, again, be fatal.

Year by year more agents arrived, by all sorts of routes. One of those who arrived by parachute provided a case which, if it had been recounted in a novel, would have aroused derision. He was an Englishman, code-name Zigzag, who has written a book broadly based on his adventures, which were, indeed, most exciting. He was a safebreaker who was in prison on Jersey when the Germans took that island. He volunteered to work for the Germans so as to get back to England, and the Germans trained him, perhaps better and more efficiently than almost any other of his level. We knew the approximate time and place of his impending arrival in Cambridgeshire from Special Intelligence and were ready to 'receive' him had he not, as he had always intended, handed himself over to the nearest policeman. That officer accompanied Zigzag to M.I.5 and, as he handed him over, he asked to speak to Tar Robertson alone. He told Tar: 'I don't know what this man may tell you, sir. He came with a German parachute, but I recognized him at once – he was in my platoon in the Irish Guards some years ago.' What writer would dare have a spy taken into the custody of a country bobby who had been in the same platoon in the army?

Zigzag also illustrates how every case has its own problems. Usually M.I.5 would naturally like to investigate and check a case before letting the agent make contact by W/T, but Zigzag warned Tar that his German spy-master had said that, if Zigzag made prompt contact right away, he would know that all was well as British red tape and bumbling would prevent that. The spy-master would be suspicious only if there was any delay. A risk was taken, which would probably have caused great difficulty if it had transpired that Zigzag was acting as a triple agent.

Less important but interesting agents were Mutt and Jeff, who arrived in the Moray Firth by seaplane from Norway, and who both had a part-Norwegian background. They were concerned largely with sabotage but they also had reporting duties.

To make them credible they had to be given some successes in their primary duties. As factory and other explosions were in fact published in our newspapers, we had to provide them with a sufficient 'bang' to get publicity. Their first sabotage was at a food dump near Wealdstone in November 1941 – at a location in the dump where no substantial damage would actually be done. This was by arrangement with the appropriate authorities but, in so populated an area, public spirited and enthusiastic outsiders tried to stifle the blaze before it rated newsworthiness.

Although the Germans were very appreciative of the result of Plan Guy Fawkes* we decided to make the next explosion in a less populated area. I had memories of an old powder factory marked on maps of the New Forest. This 'bang' was almost too good as it destroyed the evidence of sabotage, including Mutt's Norwegian pocket compass which had 'carelessly' been left to be

---

* We *did* use some almost self-evident code names for these operations – they helped to avoid confusion, they were *never* signalled and in the extremely unlikely event of an unauthorized person reading them in a document he, knowing the proper practice, would assume that Guy Fawkes could have nothing to do with an explosion!

discovered. So there was little publicity until M.I.5 sent special investigators who 'found' more clues.

The publicity resulting from these two explosions was apparently satisfactory to the Germans, when coupled with Mutt and Jeff's reports, and they dropped £400 by parachute to keep the two going (they had dropped £200 not long before). However they dropped it in the wrong place. Mutt and Jeff did not report that they had received it, so the Germans dropped another £400, another radio transmitter and some sabotage materials. Most of the last was captured S.O.E. material which caused discussion whether the Germans thought it better than theirs (it was) or did it to conceal where it came from if it was found before or after an explosion. Mutt and Jeff had to obey orders and come down from Scotland, where all this had happened, to 'damage' a factory at Bury St Edmunds. This was well publicized in the press and produced the interesting result that the Germans used the 'fact' that more than one hundred and fifty workmen had been killed very blatantly in their propaganda broadcast. But they claimed no success in damaging the factory, an interesting sidelight on their propaganda aim of injuring our morale.

There were other sabotage agents but I have mentioned these two in particular because, quite illogically, the Germans seemed to think that their 'successes' in this sphere made their reports more reliable, and from time to time they could be used for backing up naval deception.

But Garbo was the man who developed into our real star – probably out-doing even Tricycle and Tate. He was a Spaniard who was not strongly politically aligned until, according to what he told us, his brother, who happened to be in Paris when the Germans marched in, disappeared into the care of the Gestapo. Garbo then became anti-Nazi and determined on revenge.

In January 1941 he offered his services to our embassy to spy on the Germans, but was turned down. Nothing daunted, he decided to fool the Germans and offered his services to the German embassy to spy for them. He managed to persuade them that he could get sent to England by the Spaniards, and they gave him money, secret ink, cover-addresses in England and so on.

Garbo set off from Madrid, but had no means of getting

further than Lisbon where he settled down happily for some nine months. There he concocted reports about English events with the help of old guide books, out-of-date railway time-tables, English newspapers and books on England that he could pick up in Lisbon; he then sent those reports to Madrid as if a courier had brought them over from him in England.

He was brilliantly ingenious. If he found a railway line which the time-table showed had heavy traffic, he decided that it was important and reported barbed wire and pill-boxes along it. If the Germans asked him (through the 'courier') to find out if army units were being moved south from Hertfordshire, he reported that they were – and, incidentally, often reinforced that report, by 'seeing' the same troops a few days later passing through Guildford. Even more ambitiously, he 'created' two or three fictitious sub-agents to report to him from different parts of the country.

The Germans got just the information they wanted to believe and, amazingly enough, his guesses and deductions were often extraordinarily accurate. Indeed they had us worried when we read the messages as they went on over the wireless from the Abwehr to Berlin, and a lot of time was wasted on checking them – especially when other secret intelligence revealed that the Germans were making elaborate preparations to deal with a Malta convoy which Garbo's sub-agent in Liverpool had reported would sail from there. Eventually we got enough data to decide that the reports were inventions – and that someone was selling dud information to the Germans.

Garbo began to realize that he could not continue in this way for much longer. He knew virtually nothing about English customs and habits. Pounds, shillings and pence were a complete mystery to him, and his weird and wonderful expense accounts for his notional sub-agents ought to have made the Germans suspicious. He knew only one English surname – Smith! So he approached our people again – and got turned down again. But he was persistent and at last his offer, the description of his work linking him to the messages that we had seen, percolated to M.I.5, and Section B.1A decided that he would be more useful, and certainly safer from both his and our point of view, if he was a collaborator in purveying false information rather than a competitor. So in April 1942 he was smuggled over to England, where the Germans thought he had been since the previous July.

At first he was carefully examined and we played very safe in the messages. It seemed hardly credible that the Germans could really have believed the reports that he had sent, let alone have placed any reliance on them, in spite of the evidence of what they did about the convoy from Liverpool.

But soon we found that he *was* regarded quite highly, there could be no doubt about that, and B.1A decided that here was a chance to build up something really valuable – a complete high level network.

Three of his notional sub-agents could be kept on, but the one in Liverpool was notionally in a job from which he could not credibly be removed and in which he could not avoid seeing and therefore having a duty to the Germans to report things which security would prevent his actually reporting, while failure to report would eventually have blown him, and thus in all probability the whole Garbo network. Garbo therefore reported that the sub-agent had become ill, and, after some reports of the progress of his malady, that he had died. Garbo then cut out the obituary which B.1A had inserted in the *Liverpool Daily Post* and sent it to the Germans, who were courteous enough to send back a message of condolence to the widow.

I have described that 'sad event' in some detail to indicate how wonderfully 'real life' all the details of Garbo's network became – Graham Greene's delightful story *Our Man in Havana* about the spy who invented and worked a non-existent network was nothing to this real life story.*

'Tommy' Harris (the brilliant M.I.5 civilian officer who was his case-officer) and Garbo formed a close *rapport*. Four more notional sub-agents were speedily recruited to replace the dead man and reinforce the network, and gradually still more were recruited. Tommy and Garbo 'lived the life' of all these imagin-

* Sefton Delmer has given as good an account of the Garbo network as could be written by someone who had not been in actual double-agent work. It is in his book *The Counterfeit Spy* (Harper & Row). He gives Tommy Harris a false name and Garbo a false code-name because, at the time when he wrote, security demanded it.

ary sub-agents – remembering all their characteristics and foibles.
For example, if I suggested that No. 1 at, for instance, Bristol,
should report so and so, it might be that he was no use as he
never reported 'I believe' or 'I've heard that'. *He* always reported
something as a fact, but Tommy could get No. 3 to a suitable
port in a couple of days, and *he* could report a rumour. On the
other hand No. 4 who knew about a subject I wanted reported,
could not make a journey because his wife was ill. Every one of
these notional sub-agents was like a close personal friend of
Tommy and Garbo and lived in their minds.

The Germans' belief in Garbo was proved again and again.
The brilliant handling of this network by all concerned paid
dividends. Our first firm evidence of the strength of the Abwehr's
belief in Garbo was when he had been given a W/T set and they
sent him the same high-level cipher as was used between two
Abwehr stations. When the cipher was changed they sent him
the new one, which incidentally saved Bletchley Park a bit of
trouble!

He, like Tricycle and Tate and some others, lasted until
V.E. Day – indeed he had not long before that recruited a
notional Wren rating working in Lord Louis Mountbatten's
Supreme H.Q. in the Far East, in case deception out there required some reinforcement. She was to report by letter to Garbo,
the information would then go by W/T to Lisbon and on to
Berlin. There it would be given to the Japanese Military Attaché
who would radio it to Tokyo. The German faith in Garbo was
so great that they considered that one of his sub-agents (remember they were paying all these sub-agents) would get enough
solid information, not mere out-dated ship movement reports, to
make all this worthwhile. This scheme did not, in fact, ever get
going as Germany surrendered before it could.

The fact that these three stars and some others remained un-
blown to the end was a wonderful feat considering the important
deceptions that they helped to put over. Some of the agents and
sub-agents had to disappear in order to make our operation
credible. Some notionally got ill and died, some, notionally in
the Services, were posted abroad. Some just gave up – as free
agents often did – reporting that they were getting frightened.

Some gave up because the Germans could not get money to them. Some just suddenly stopped reporting as if they had been caught, if their 'arrest' would not compromise others that we needed to keep on. One of these was Zigzag, after he had had an exciting career in sabotage and reporting. He was a patriotic man and had great courage, even going back for further training by the Germans in Norway, before being parachuted back to us again. He brought back with him a great deal of valuable information about many things – the results of our bombing in various towns and cities that he had visited in Germany and new weapons including the V-bombs and 'radio controlled rockets' – also his view that Goebbels' propaganda had persuaded. the Germans that London was as badly damaged as Berlin. But German morale was falling in spite of that, while German naval morale was also very low owing to British anti-U-boat devices and their losses.

He had a questionnaire of great intelligence interest showing German anxiety about our anti-U-boat Asdic (under-water detectors); also about weapons and devices which we were able to deduce would be useful against V-bombs. They also wanted to know the whereabouts of American airfields as they thought that it was the Americans who were bombing German towns.

The Germans had given him £6,000, besides two wireless sets and cameras, and had promised him a princely sum in German money when he finally returned to Germany after a successful mission.

It looked as if the Germans valued Zigzag highly after the special training and extremely generous treatment that they had given him. We felt that we had another really first-class agent in the making, but unfortunately he began 'to talk', giving hints of what he was doing to friends. So he had to be closed down, just as would have happened by arrest in real life!

More Naval Deceptions

In addition to major strategic and general deceptions which met specific requirements such as the V-bombs and our various invasions, each Service used the double agents for their own individual needs.

Early in 1942 the Twenty Committee decided that it would help if the Service departments were each to produce a directive on its programme, thus giving advance warning to B.1A about what was to come – apart from any sudden *ad hoc* deception. It would also give the general line that each Service would wish to take in answering questions put to agents by the Germans, as well as in providing and approving the day to day contents of their agents' messages and the background of these messages – what we called 'chicken-feed'.

Contrary to its later outstanding courage in tackling the V.1 problem the Home Defence Executive (speaking for all the civilian side) was pusillanimous enough to be completely negative – 'don't be accurate especially where we might indicate possible targets for bombing or bomb-damage'. Their only positive suggestion was pretty useless. It was to write up civilian morale. What spy would go out of his way to report high morale in what was, to him, the enemy country?

The War Office also wanted weapons, morale and everything else to be played up – they did not think the time ripe for trying any active deceptions. The Home Forces Command were positively unhelpful. According to them, as we had no definite military plans and as we had to give some true information in order to keep the agents going, we should abandon the whole project, winding up all the agents and thus making the Germans try to set up a new spy system. Fortunately these views were overwhelmingly outvoted.

The Air Ministry had produced a policy in late 1941 which helped B.1A immensely to get over to the Germans a picture of industrious and observant spies. Broadly it was to produce an impression of lots of aircraft and airfields, but poor quality aircraft, poor quality training, and many badly defended airfields, to try to draw attacks away from the many towns and factories, which could not be defended, on to the airfields, which could. But in 1942 they produced nothing.

Ignoring all this my directive from Uncle John was to build up as many agents as possible in anticipation of major deceptions, providing as much accurate information as we could do without real risk. In 1942 we really got going on a steady campaign to increase the number of merchantmen and warships being built. The merchant ship reports were for a general 'build up' purpose; the warships so that we could hope to put over a threat of increased convoy escorts, U-boat hunting groups, and major warships. By a mass of small details we managed after a time always to have in service more warships than in fact existed. From several in the case of smaller ships to one each in the case of capital ships and aircraft carriers.

We had, all along, to cope with the major difficulty caused by the activities of neutral diplomats. These were a headache, both to normal security and also to any deception operations. Most of the Spanish and some of the Japanese attachés were active in their collection of information which could be of benefit to the Germans, often in answer to instructions passed on from the Germans through either Franco's ministers or the Japanese Embassy in Berlin. The German and Japanese diplomatic, and the Abwehr, wireless traffic disclosed this.

A danger of a different kind was caused by the pro-Allied attachés. After all, they had a job to do, and had to report to their own governments even when those governments as a whole were also pro-Allied there would almost inevitably be some pro-

Germans among the ministers and officials of the government concerned. And there was unfortunately a tendency among some British 'top brass' both Service and civilian, to be careless in their revelations. 'Oh, Colonel X is all right, he's as pro-British as I am – he even hunts with the Quorn.'

Apart from that general danger there was an extra risk intrinsic to a deception about warship building. Shipbuilding is a long-term job, lasting some years, and the hulls are very big and visible from afar. One of our double agents might report notional shipbuilding, perhaps one cruiser where there was none, or two where there was in fact one. Then a neutral diplomat might pass the same yard and see from the railway that there was one hull or none visible, or a hull that was far less complete than we had reported and pass the true information on to his government. Then, of course, it would reach Berlin.

There was also another complication arising from the fact that the Admiralty Press Division, very rightly from the point of view of naval and civilian morale, usually gave the names of ships which had taken part in some operation. It would have been damagingly suspicious if the notional ships that we had reported as being completed, or nearly completed, never appeared in the news. We minimized this difficulty, and the sort of careless disclosures to friendly neutrals that I have mentioned, by a simple process. Warships were always named in advance in the unpublished building programme, so we always used the next name or names for our extra ships. For instance in the Illustrious class of aircraft carriers, *Invincible* notionally went into service well before she actually did.

Somehow we managed to get away with this operation, and there was some confirmation that both the Germans and Japanese swallowed it. The Commander-in-Chief Far East Fleet in 1942 had not been able to obtain another aircraft carrier for the Indian Ocean as none could be spared and he asked that we should try to convince the Japanese that there were two there instead of none. Owing to our phoney shipbuilding we apparently convinced the Germans that we had enough aircraft carriers to be able, realistically, to spare two – and when Tate reported that two had sailed for the East, the Germans passed this information on as fact to the Japanese in Berlin who transmitted it to Tokyo.

Incidentally, we backed up this deception when carrying out another deception of a more scientific nature. We had been asked to try to convince the Germans that we had developed electrical devices which enabled aircraft to land on aircraft carriers at night. This we had done, and we now supported both deceptions by a report that an expert was being flown to Durban because this new gear on one of the carriers en route to the Far East had developed some teething trouble and no one out there had the requisite knowledge to put it right.

Shortly after this we had an urgent 'flap' to cope with. We suddenly learnt that one of the aircraft carriers that we had 'in fact' by now got firmly into the Indian Ocean was going to call at Gibraltar on her passage home from an operation in the Atlantic. She would certainly be spotted and reported to Berlin. After urgent discussions the visit was cancelled at the last minute.

This illustrates how essential it was that, on top of all my other work, I should see our own operational signals and plans daily – and how lucky it was that V.C.N.S. and the Directors of the Operations Divisions were convinced enough of the existing and potential value of deception to be willing to help.

The warship building deception had another quite distinct facet which also was a long-term one. We had been particularly asked to build up the number of available 'Woolworth' carriers as much as we could. These were merchant ship hulls fitted as mini-aircraft carriers for convoy escort duties and, as they were mostly built in America, notional extra ships could not be reported on by agents over here while under construction. This part of the deception had therefore to be carried out almost entirely by notional leaks from Service personnel.

Two other long-term operations were connected with the badly battered North Russian convoys. Apart from a number of individually small bits of misinformation that the Commander-in-Chief Home Fleet wanted the Germans to believe about his ships or operations, he always wanted them to think that he had more ships than he actually had. Also, once the Americans were in the war, he wanted us to report the arrival of American ships during the gaps between convoys so as to keep the Germans on the stretch. The second major facet came somewhat later when he conceived the idea that the Germans might be influenced in their tactics if they believed that the close escort forces, spotted from the air as being lamentably weak, were reinforced by a covering escort of submarines.

These deceptions had to be done carefully if we were not to blow our agents through the Germans learning that they were either false or tendentious. The main burden was carried out through Tate and, while we had no knowledge whether the deceptions were successful, at least they did not damage his reputation with his German masters, indeed quite the reverse.

Having indicated the sort of information that Tate was passing, this makes it easier to explain the way that the Germans had been persuaded that he was getting it. Early on in my deception work I felt sure that we would want to pass some naval misinformation that could only be obtained from someone within the Service, including some which could only come from a really high level. My first idea was a notional person in the Admiralty – but such a person in a position where he could plausibly learn some of the very high level things that I might want him to transmit to the Germans would have to be in a position to know far too much. If he reported some very important phoney things, how could he fail to report lots of other real things which could not safely be passed to the Germans but which they would soon learn? It occurred to me that someone like a confidential clerk in the Admiralty could be lent to the American Naval Headquarters in London in a job where she could only learn what the Admiralty passed to the Americans. The Admiralty could, notionally but plausibly, pass to them some Top Secret naval movement or naval development, which could be either true or untrue, and yet not pass to them others.

After discussing this idea with Tar Robertson of B.1A, he worked out a first-rate scheme whereby Tate, who was a very personable man, should notionally get off with a notional girl called Mary (who had this job) and become intimate with her. She was not a traitress but *extremely* indiscreet to her boy friend when she could show off about the importance of her job. Had she been a traitress she would have given Tate far too much information for our safety if she was to remain credible to the Germans. Also it would be quite natural for her to have a number of British naval officer friends to whom she would notionally introduce Tate, and they would, in their turn, introduce him to others.

I then reported the idea to Uncle John. It was just his cup of tea and he fixed up for me to see Admiral Stark, the United States Navy Commander-in-Chief in Europe, whose H.Q. was in Grosvenor Square. He was most helpful and, after Uncle John's build-up, was willing to trust me to pass to the Germans information and misinformation about the U.S. naval movements in European waters in exactly the same way as I did about our own Navy. If we had been successful and safe as regards our Navy there was no more and no less risk for the Americans. He did not ask how we did it and did not ask for any reports from me unless D.N.I. considered that he should be told something. A really 'big' man. Later, when Admiral Kirk succeeded Admiral Stark, I had a similar interview with him, and the arrangement was continued unaltered.

We also developed a minor, but nevertheless very useful and effective, means of backing up quite a number of deceptions. This method could not, from its nature, be used by itself to put over a full-scale deception but could back up and seem to the Germans to confirm one that had been put over by double agents.

We had learnt from Special Intelligence that the Abwehr in Spain had managed to tap one of the telephone lines used by our Embassy in Madrid. It seemed that the listening in was done by an Abwehr member but it might have been done by a Spanish telephone operator who had been bribed. In any case the Abwehr wireless traffic made it clear that a senior Spanish official had been 'squared' to allow the original tapping of the line.

After some discussion it was decided that we could be allowed to take advantage of this breach by the Spaniards of proper diplomatic practice, especially as it was impossible to make a formal diplomatic protest as that would compromise our source of knowledge. The Naval Attaché was not to do anything positive himself. If he received 'instructions' over the line, he was not to implement them.

For instance, we would 'instruct' him, from time to time, to 'counter a rumour which seemed to be gaining credence'. One example out of many comes to my mind: as part of the effort to deter the Japanese from pressing their advance on Singapore too speedily after Pearl Harbor, we were instructed to give as much indication as possible that our naval build-up in the East was proceeding quickly. So, during a conversation with the attaché on ordinary matters, there was added 'if you hear the rumour in Madrid which is current here that Tom Phillips (Admiral Sir Tom Phillips) has quarrelled with the Admiralty and the Prime Minister over policy, and has been sacked, you might deny it – it's not fair on him. In fact he's got his dearest wish and left to command the Far East Fleet which has been increased.' In fact he *had* been moved from Vice-Chief of the Naval Staff to that appointment, but to announce it publicly at that stage would have been contrary to general policy and would have created future complications. The attaché of course behaved scrupulously properly and did nothing. It was the Abwehr who behaved improperly, bugged the conversation and reported to Berlin for us.

By the same means we were able to give direct to the Abwehr quite a number of what must have seemed to them to be incautious leaks in the course of routine administrative conversations. Among these were such remarks as that the speaker had run into Bill Smith who had got a spot of unexpected leave as the underwater torpedo tubes of H.M.S. *Duke of York*, in which he was serving, were being improved; and that another speaker was very amused when he heard someone on the bus saying that 'Woolworth' ships were the old American destroyers that Roosevelt had given to Churchill, instead of mini-aircraft carriers – he thought that must be caused because there were such a number of them coming into convoy escort duties.

The first of these was, of course, to back up the deception that the Commander-in-Chief Home Fleet had asked us to put over, and the other, not very amusing anecdote was to counter a German impression revealed by some of the questions to double agents. These questions told them to find out what 'Woolworth' referred to in connection with ships and indicated that the Ger-

mans had picked up the word in a 'leaky' conversation by a seaman in Lisbon – and had put the wrong interpretation on it. On
the other hand we did not want any misunderstanding to pre-
judice our exaggeration of the building of mini-aircraft carriers
before we could plausibly answer the question through the double
agents.

Another very long-term double agent operation concerned
anti-torpedo nets fitted to some merchant ships and used to protect anchorages. The Germans were insatiable in their quest for
information on this subject and kept sending questions to many
agents of every level whom they thought might gain some knowledge about it, even including a multi-part question on the subject in Tricycle's high-level questionnaire for his mission to
America. They could see nets fitted to some ships when they
visited neutral ports but they wanted to know all sorts of details,
for instance whether they were used at sea and, if so, by how
much they reduced the ship's speed, what proportion of ships
were fitted with them and, of course, details of their construction.
Also whether the nets to protect anchorages were different and,
if so, in what respects.

This was obviously one of the many subjects on which I had
to get guidance. It transpired that what we wanted the Germans
to believe was easy to define, even if it was much more difficult
to decide which agent could credibly find out which detail, and
how misinformation could also be worked into his reports. With
so many agents reporting on one subject (and many were in a
position in which they could not credibly fail to find out *something*) it was a problem with which the able case-officers were
faced to avoid getting the agents' 'wires crossed' so that one compromised another – yet avoiding all appearing to have got their
information from a single source.

There was, however, another really secret point about which the
Germans never asked specifically. Apparently our nets caught
the torpedoes by the tail, and not by the head as in the first war.
We were told that it was *most* important that the Germans should
not realize this. No information that we gave must lead the Germans to deduce this and we must try to lead them away from doing
so. There is some indication that we may have been successful

as we were told that they never adopted the reasonably simple alteration to their torpedoes which would have defeated this system. That particular German failure is unlikely to have been due to stupidity as the other improvements and alterations made to their torpedoes were most ingenious.

From the questions that some agents received, the Germans showed that they were puzzled how we were detecting so many U-boats. Having apparently accepted our reports lowering the supposed efficiency of our radar, they were puzzled and anxious to learn how we spotted them. From our point of view it was *vital* that they should not find out because it was based on our deciphering of their U-boat signals. However, as so often happened, the Germans helped us.

Perhaps because of the ingenuity of the bolometers that they wanted to use in the Gibraltar Straits they began to wonder whether we were using some infra-red device. This was a godsend and we jumped at it. Professor Gollin helped us, with great ingenuity, in the devising of reports that would foster this belief. He even produced a paint which gave rather less reaction than normal paint to infra-red apparatus. We then had one of the agents, a merchant seaman, notionally get a scraping of the paint from a ship-yard worker who had shown it to his pals, including the agent, in a pub with the story that it was very new, and secret, and was being put on our submarines. The ship-yard worker, and the agent, had no idea why a new type of paint was being used or why it was secret and had come to the conclusion that it *might* be a new and much more efficient anti-fouling paint. The agent then dropped a bit of the scraping off in Lisbon when he next docked there. We never got any further news of this paint as, obviously, it could not be sent to Germany by wireless, so that we could decipher the message, but had to be sent by land. We hope that they analysed the paint. It was clearly not antifouling and Gollin was confident that a capable scientific analysis would reveal the anti-infra-red properties. If we were using such paint the Germans would be likely to deduce that it was because they might develop as good infra-red anti-submarine detectors as we had and use them against our submarines.

We added to this deception and tried to increase the worries of U-boat commanders, by notionally improving the efficiency, range, etc., of our anti-submarine detectors. Further to add to their worries we passed misinformation about our new-type mines, particularly one called Mark XXIV. We got no check on the success of these deceptions.

Yet another opportunity to increase their worries was given to us when the Germans picked up from careless talk by merchant seamen the fact that we had fitted a new anti-submarine weapon of some kind to destroyers, frigates and corvettes, and that it was called Hedgehog. Several of the double agents were asked for details of this weapon, its construction and capabilities. I consulted the appropriate people and it was decided that we should let the Germans know that it was what it in fact was – a weapon which fired depth charges forward instead of dropping them astern as had always been done in the past. Also that, while we should not disclose any details of their design and construction, we should notionally increase their range and explosive effect and more important, try to convince the Germans that they were fitted with proximity fuses which would go off on a near miss without actual impact, and so did not depend on a depth-setting in order to time their explosion as did ordinary depth charges.

We were delighted to get these instructions. Not only was it a very realistic brief, as agents could quite reasonably be expected to learn these general facts even if they were not in a position to get details of construction, but it also gave us an opportunity which we wanted in the specifically double-cross campaign.

We knew from Special Intelligence that the Germans had recruited an agent in Spain whom they had code-named Ostro. For a short while the messages that we read when they were transmitted to Berlin caused us considerable concern. They purported to be coming from England and they seemed to be the first sign of an agent operating from here who was not under our control. However, checks on the content of the messages, as they were being passed on from the Abwehr in Madrid to Berlin, soon showed that they consisted of general facts gleaned quite intelligently from English newspapers and broadcasts available in Lisbon – only slightly 'doctored' and edited. Anything else that the messages contained was wholly inaccurate guesswork. We surmised, as it turned out correctly, that Ostro was an enterprising free-lance gaining a dishonest penny by purporting to have a network of informants reporting to him from England, while really paraphrasing and adding to published news and just inventing the rest, mostly about the sailings of merchant ships from various ports; he was in fact a Czech living in Lisbon. Nevertheless he was a danger in that one of his inventions might turn out, quite by chance, to be correct about something which needed to be secret, or his reports, where they differed from those of our double agents, might lessen German faith in the latter – at any rate the lower grade ones. So we wanted to discredit him, and here was a golden opportunity.

Ostro, like our double agents, had been asked what Hedgehog was, and he had firmly and definitely attributed the code-name to something quite different. Now our agents, one after the other, could report the truth, and the Germans were bound to learn in due course that it *was* the truth. This part of the manoeuvre went well. Gradually Ostro's reports ceased to be sent on to Berlin and all of our agents received praise from the Abwehr.

Then the Germans gave us a further opportunity. Apparently U-boats had reported that, when attacked by Hedgehogs, they had heard a lesser bang before the main explosion of the depth charges and they wanted to know what caused these smaller bangs. Enquiries by us revealed that the lesser bang was, in fact, the explosion of the propellant charge which fired the Hedgehog depth charges forward, transmitted through the hull of the ship and then on through the water. However, this gave us an opportunity to foster the idea that there was a proximity fuse. Professor Gollin devised a story, with full details, of a smaller projectile which was fired at the same time as the big ones. By means which I, as a layman, could not fully understand, this smaller projectile was attracted towards the U-boat and was then detonated by a proximity fuse, and that, in its turn, set off the depth charges a few seconds afterwards.

It so happened that Zigzag was in a position where he could credibly gain this information and he duly put over my layman's version, as amended and improved by Professor Gollin. After passing the information on to the German Navy the Abwehr came back to Zigzag with much praise and an insistent demand that he should get more details.

He now notionally excelled himself as the ex-safe-breaker. He reported that he had broken into a naval store where he had photographed one of these weapons which, incidentally, we code-named Squid to cover a different new weapon of that name. The photograph was actually one of a real Hedgehog depth charge against which we had put a 'one foot rule' which was in fact 36 inches long – so that the Squid with a small bang appeared to be one third of the size of a really damaging Hedgehog depth charge.

Zigzag passed over a full 'layman's description' of what he had seen, but the Germans wanted the photo. So Zigzag notionally suborned a seaman and then transmitted the following proposition to the Germans. He would put the negative into a frenchletter, and then he would put that into a tin of Epsom Salts. The sailor, who was not a traitor, would be under the impression that he was 'merely' smuggling drugs!

After they had received the photo the Abwehr were avid for full details of the fuse. Gollin therefore elicited the help of another professor who worked in the development of underwater weapons. Together they constructed a suitably altered fuse and produced a letter describing it. This was written on the second professor's official notepaper and purported to be part of a discussion with yet another professor about the development of the fuse, work which they purported to be engaged on together. Zigzag notionally broke in again and photographed both of these. He transmitted details by his wireless and was about to send the negatives by the same route as before when we had 'notionally' to arrest him.

We never found out what the assessment of this information by the German Navy was, but the actions of the Abwehr made it seem that it must have been very favourable. In any case the 'arrest' of Zigzag must have added to its credibility.

A lot of our deceptions were, of course, connected with the U-boat war. U-boats had developed a tactic whereby, when being hunted by Asdic, they blew a charge of air out of a torpedo tube. This formed a mass of bubbles which might be followed by the Asdic, enabling the U-boat to creep slowly away. Our hunting vessels were frequently foxed by this tactic and we were asked to discourage its use, *if* we could. After discussion with Professor Gollin it was decided that it was at any rate *theoretically* possible that a development of Asdic might eventually be able to detect reflections of the escaping U-boat bouncing off the mass of bubbles, and thereby learn the direction it was taking. Tate notionally entertained the commanding officer of a new frigate who had sunk a U-boat by means of this device and, with his tongue loosened by drink, boasted about his success. 'The bloody fools didn't realize that they were *helping* us by blowing their bloody bubbles. He's forever blowing bubbles, pretty bubbles in the water.' Tate linked this to the report of a U-boat which had actually been sunk, sunk in spite of having blown bubbles, in which tactic she must have been trained.

A rocket-propelled depth charge deception arose in the following way. At one period the improved types of U-boats were beginning to go deeper when they were hunted, a tactic which was causing problems, and we were asked to try to discourage it. So one of the agents notionally picked up a story that our successes were due to our having managed to fit rockets to a new type of depth charge, and that this caused them to sink deep quickly – and, of course, the denser water at greater depths increased the violence and range of the shock wave when they exploded, while the water pressure had already increased the vulnerability of the U-boat hull.

Minor deceptions included weighting favourably the answers to questions put to double agents and short-term deceptions to cover some particular event or some weapon during its development period, or sometimes to induce a not very important belief by the enemy. One of these was concerned with the Monsters, as we called the *Queen Elizabeth* and the *Queen Mary*, and certain other fast ships which usually sailed unescorted. Churchill had put an absolute ban on any publication of the fact that the Monsters were sailing at all, an odd error in someone of such enormous common sense. He ignored the fact that, not only had pictures been published which showed him on board what was obviously one of the 'Queens', but both sailed again and again from the centre of New York where they were visible to thousands.

The Admiralty had, naturally, always been worried about the safety of the Monsters and other unescorted ships which depended almost entirely on their speed and the brilliance of the evasive routeing carried out by the O.I.C. We were asked to help, but all that we could think of was to pass to the Germans reports of the fitting of depth charges, Hedgehogs, U-boat detection devices and so on to such ships. Apparently this was thought good enough to cause the Admiralty to persuade Churchill to withdraw his ban, even though he was not told any details of our double agent work.

Every now and again, in order to conceal the actual target of an operation – say the Dieppe raid – if the preparations or the concentration of men and ships were to leak or if our old bugbears, the neutral diplomats, picked up the fact that something was afoot, we were asked to try to give the Germans the idea that we were going to attack somewhere else. The cover target as it was called was often Norway, which was geographically well away from the real one.

Obviously we could not use the double agents for this purpose, except for some low grade agents who might report that they had picked up some rumour or bit of gossip. The virtual certainty of depreciating the high credibility that the Germans had for the better agents, if we were to use them for such a purpose, was clearly unacceptable.

On one occasion we had what we felt to be a bright idea. We circularized the Registrars of Shipping in the appropriate ports asking them to compile a list of trawlermen and merchant seamen who were familiar with the coastal waters and fjords of Norway.

A number complied but some wrote back indignantly pointing out that the enquiries that they would have to make among the men would be bound to leak and would be certain to compromise the security of any operation which was being contemplated against occupied Norway.

We could not reply that that was just what we wanted to

E

happen and had to write back thanking these Registrars for pointing out this danger, leaving them more convinced than ever of the incompetence and insecurity of the Admiralty.

This brings me to a deception operation which we did *not* carry out, one which raises ethical questions. My scheme, to which we gave the code-name Iago, was designed to 'frame' one of the most successful U-boat captains operating out of Bordeaux. If successful it would not only have removed one of the top scorers in the sinking of our merchant ships, and thus have saved many ships, lives and cargoes, but it would also have struck heavily at the morale of the U-boat crews, which at that time was high. Also it would have helped enormously in the vital concealment of our reading of the U-boat signals on which so much depended.

'C', our Secret Intelligence Service, should arrange to send from France or Spain to this captain a commercial type calendar of the very sexy pin-up girl kind that the captain would be likely to hang up in his quarters; this would have a message on the back, written in secret ink which had been developed and then allowed to fade again. The message would thank the captain for the last of his reports that had been received about U-boat sailings and changes in strategy. He would not suspect the presence of the message, invisible until it was again developed, but, even if he was so unsailorlike as not to hang up the calendar, it would not really matter very much.

The next step would be for a message to be sent to a suitable agent of 'C''s in France who was known to us to be blown, so that any message sent to him was bound to be read by the Germans. This would instruct him to send to the captain some money and a scarf impregnated with the same secret ink as had been used for the message on the calendar – the usual way in which to send replenishments of secret ink to an agent who, on receiving the cloth, would soak it so as to melt the dried crystals and then squeeze it into a bottle.

On reading the message, the Gestapo would start enquiries and the unfortunate captain would be arrested, even if he had not kept the calendar. To make his conviction absolutely certain we would follow with a message to him from 'C', in the same secret ink, thanking him for, say, the information that he had sent about the passages which the U-boats used through the German defensive minefields and asking him for clarification of some details. The captain would be court-martialled and almost certainly shot as a traitor.

After discussion my plan was turned down flat on the 'it's not cricket' principle. 'We don't assassinate people.' It was obvious casuistry to argue that *we* would not be shooting the U-boat captain – the Germans would do it.

If we could have got someone to blow Hitler up surely we would have jumped at the opportunity and saved thousands of lives? Would getting somebody to shoot the U-boat captain be wrong because it would save fewer lives? If so, was it because he had killed and would kill fewer unarmed people than Hitler did? If so, what are the deciding numbers? One can go on putting such questions about whether the decision not to implement my scheme was right or wrong and, in deciding, one must bear in mind the conditions and situation in 1942 and 1943. We were fighting for our very lives, for the preservation of freedom in the world, and damned near being beaten. I sometimes think that it was right and sometimes that it was wrong.

12

The Start of Major Deceptions

Something that we learnt from Special Intelligence was that it was impossible to put over a changing deception. When an Abwehr out-station got a series of reports indicating A, drew the deduction that the truth was A, and reported A to Berlin, and then started to get reports indicating B, they would be reluctant to change their belief. For some time they would, perhaps even honestly, judge the later reports to be mistaken. Then they would be reluctant to reveal to Berlin that they had been wrong, as mistakes so often caused the spy-master to disappear from our traffic, probably to the Russian front. We often saw reports of something (not necessarily strategic) that we had put over continuing to be sent to Berlin for some considerable time after we had stopped sending such reports. This was probably done by the Abwehr out-station to reinforce the truth of our earlier reports and show how efficient the spy-master was so that he should stay in the nice safe posting of Lisbon or Madrid.

Berlin would have difficulty in knowing which contradictory reports to believe. They had had no Admiral John Godfrey to institute a grading system, and almost all reports were labelled 'from a usually reliable agent', virtually the only exception being those from agents who were identified by their German code-names and known to have star value, such as our trio of stars Garbo, Tricycle and Tate.

While we were gaining this knowledge, deception had been found to be most useful in the Middle East where General Wavell especially had been 'deception minded'. They had very few double agents there and none of really high grade, but much success had been gained with solid deception like dummy tanks and an increase of radio traffic from the wrong place.

The Chiefs of Staff suddenly became impressed with the idea of deception, and instituted a new system, one which was to prove of immense value when the mistakes had been ironed out, but which was very ill-considered to start with. For good reasons they had no knowledge of the extent of the double agents system and they had not the slightest idea of how a deception could actually be put over. Worst of all, they did not appreciate what I have described as the cardinal rule.

They appointed Colonel 'Johnny' Bevan as the first effective head of a new body called the London Controlling Section (L.C.S.), which was to be a subordinate inter-service body of the Chiefs of Staff Committee. Not only did none of these officers have experience of the difficult art of deception but the task that they were given was virtually an impossible one.

First of all the L.C.S., being formally constituted, had none of the freedom of action that the W-board had given to the Twenty Committee. They always had to get authority to put over any strategic deception, even though, thank heaven, the Chiefs of Staff did not require that they should give details of the means by which they proposed to do it.

This status of the L.C.S. did bring an immense advantage in that they had a direct and immediate contact with the planners and the eventual commanders of any operation. But even this brought an enormous disadvantage on the first occasion that the L.C.S. operated, before Johnny Bevan got it on to the right lines.

The Twenty Committee had pressed for the cover target for Operation Torch, the landing in North Africa, to be an expedition to Dakar, a realistically practical cover target in view of the failure of de Gaulle's previous attack there. We had no doubt that we could put this over successfully. The most important reason was that the Germans were ready to believe this story. They considered that the Allies must launch an operation soon and were anxious to learn where. Therefore, as we knew from Special Intelligence, they had themselves put out a *ballon d'éssai*

that we were going to attack Dakar. As a result, some of their
agents abroad, in the Peninsula and elsewhere, picked up rumours of Dakar as a target. These were passed on, and with sur-
prising faith the Abwehr began to believe the reports. We would
have been delighted to join in their chorus as agents might well
get good marks even after the landings in North Africa. They
would have got it right that it was a French-speaking target with
a hot climate, and a high level agent could even have indicated
Dakar as the particular target without losing credit as long as
he had taken care only to pass indications of hot climate, a
French-speaking target as hard fact, and Dakar as a matter of
inference or on the basis of loose talk.

But the L.C.S., as a formal body, had to ask the Chiefs of
Staff for approval of any proposed cover target. The Chiefs of
Staff in turn felt that they must ask the Foreign Office. The
Foreign Office, believe it or not, turned the proposal down, 'be-
cause of the difficulties it might cause with the French'.

No one could understand the thinking behind that ruling. One
presumes that there must have been some. If the distribution of
Special Intelligence in the Foreign Office was even barely efficient, whoever made that decision ought to have been on the
list and ought to have known that, if the Germans had a way
of making trouble between us and the French by means of their
agents' reports, they already had plenty of such reports with
which to do it.

Even if that person in the Foreign Office did not see Special
Intelligence, as he should have done to carry out his job properly, and thought that the Germans could harm us with the
French if they had spy reports that we were going to attack
Dakar, his decision still seemed senseless. Very soon the French
would know that the Germans were wrong as we would in fact
land, not in Dakar, but in North Africa. The decision seemed
still more senseless when one bore in mind that North Africa and
Dakar were both equally French possessions.

I have stressed this at some length as it was the first indication
of many of the difficulties caused by deception being put on to
a formal basis, and an indication of how wise the W-board was
to keep such matters informal and in the hands, on both the

working and the supervisory level, of people who knew what they were doing.

The Chiefs of Staff then gave the L.C.S. a directive which would have been impossible to implement, even if it had not been imposed on them before they had gained any experience. The Chiefs of Staff picked on Norway as the cover target – an expedition to liberate that country – but agreed that somewhere else must be found to cover the fact that shipping, assault craft and so on would be reported by the many Spanish agents working in Gibraltar.

After Dakar had been vetoed, we had suggested a notional reverse-Dunkirk to Malta – that convoys to Malta of big ships had suffered such losses that we were going to try to disperse the German and Italian attacks by sending some ships and a mass of small craft spread all over the Mediterranean in the hope that more supplies would get through to Malta in that way with fewer losses.

The Chiefs of Staff then compromised on a combination of those two cover targets: while the expedition to North Africa was preparing in the United Kingdom, we should try to convince the Germans that it was going to liberate Norway. Then, when it left the United Kingdom, the cover plan was to be changed to the 'reverse-Dunkirk' to Malta that we had suggested. This set the unfortunate Johnny Bevan a hopeless task.

Firstly the directive ignored the basic principle of deception – that sudden switches are impossible to put over. Secondly, if we had implemented the first part of the directive, an attack on occupied Norway, in the normal way we would certainly have blown all the double agents, wasting them before they were *really* needed to put over the cover plan for our cross-Channel assault. After all, to make reports of the preparation of an expedition to a colder, mountainous country to the north credible would have required those reports to be of a kind which, when the expedition landed in Africa, would be revealed to have been either wildly incompetent or, much more likely, deliberately false.

However, we were able to help in this respect to a small degree. It was considered that the early stages of the long voyage of the convoys from the United Kingdom and the United States would be at considerable risk. In those circumstances it was decided that the Home Fleet should actually put to sea at the appropriate time and sail north-west towards Norway. There was, however, one major defect in this idea. The movement, though real, would be useless if the Germans did not know in which direction the Fleet had sailed, and there was every probability that they would not do so. The reconnaissance flights over its base were infrequent and, according to the established pattern, a flight was unlikely at the required time.

We decided that we could help at this point. Tate duly reported to the Germans that he had met, at a dinner party with some officers of the battleship H.M.S. *Anson*, two American officers from the battleships U.S.S. *Alabama* and the U.S.S. *South Dakota*. In the conversation they had mentioned that five American destroyers were with them and that they had been warned to have cold-weather clothing – the general atmosphere was that they expected action very soon. All this was quite within the general pattern of the life that Tate was living and, while the Germans would draw the inference that an attack of some sort on Norway was likely, its failure to materialize would not harm Tate's reputation if the ships did sail towards Norway and were spotted doing so – in fact, quite the reverse – even if they did subsequently turn back.

This report by Tate was backed up by a much lower grade double agent, Cobweb, who was at that time reporting to the Germans by wireless from Iceland. He sent an accurate message that two cruisers had sailed north from that island.

The Germans swallowed these reports and special reconnaissances were flown off the naval base at Scapa Flow and off Iceland which duly spotted and reported the ships on a course headed towards Norway, and a state of alarm was put into operation off the Norwegian coast.

The Germans continued to be flooded with the reports of an impending attack on Dakar. When they did arrive, there was no reason for the reports to stop. But at that stage rumours were started in Gibraltar that they were to supply Malta and a few of these were passed on to Berlin. Gradually the number increased. Then suddenly the Governor of Gibraltar, General Mason McFarlane, decided off his own bat to lend a hand. I have no doubt that he may well have been a fine soldier, but as an intelligence brain, one wonders.

He decided that the way to make his contribution to the deception was to give a broadcast on the garrison public address system to the effect, 'I'm sure that all of you will put your backs into this and work all hours, and work really hard. We've had it easy here, while your pals in Malta have been bombed and bombed and bombed – and on short rations. Now you can help them. Go to it.' Fine, vigorous stuff. But the immediate result was that Abwehr Madrid, not being nearly as stupid as the general, immediately informed Berlin that the Dunkirk type Malta-convoy was a plant (if it had been the true operation, no public broadcast could conceivably have been made). Fortunately the Germans stuck to their Dakar theory and the North African landings were a complete surprise to the Germans, but no thanks to anything done by the L.C.S. or us – or the general.

Incidentally, this episode might have had me court-martialled. Not many people besides me had got the Special Intelligence and, through the I.S.S.B. documents, the Governor's broadcast. I realized that if we were not to risk having our future deception plans frustrated, and probably also our agents blown, this sort of thing must not be repeated.

By hindsight, of course, I should have reported formally to D.N.I. What I did do – it seemed so obvious, simple and quick – was to give to Ginger Lewis, the naval representative on the I.S.S.B., a chit on the lines of the last few paragraphs, and to ask him to get his War Office opposite number to see if he couldn't get them to stop 'half-witted generals' (I think those were the words I used) from butting in as amateur deceivers into an art that they didn't understand. He thought that the actual chit would impress the army representative and passed the chit on. The soldier was also impressed by the force of the facts in the chit and passed it on to the Director of Military Intelligence.

The result was that I was summoned to Uncle John's room where, looking his fiercest, he handed me a letter he had received from the Director of Military Intelligence. This enclosed

my chit and stated that it was intolerable that a Lieutenant-
Commander R.N.V.R., should write in those terms of a general
and demanding, fiercely, that Lieutenant-Commander Montagu
should be disciplined. When I had read it there was a pause
while I tried to think of something that I could say. Then a smile
came on to Uncle John's face. He said, 'Try to tone down your
chits – and, if the facts necessitate anything as strong as these did,
make sure where the chit goes. To me for instance. You can go.'

Apart from that lesson, other lessons on a much more important level would be learnt from the mistakes in the cover-
plans for Operation Torch. Fortunately Major Masterman and
Colonel Bevan were both very able and sensible men. Johnny
Bevan saw that a good co-ordination with the Twenty Committee was necessary and realized that that Committee and B.1A
had a lot of experience and expertise in its double agent work –
and that that form of deception could be invaluable to him.
And J. C. Masterman was not only a wise man, full of common
sense, but also supremely tactful.

Another snag arose owing to the form of the London Controlling Section's brief which gave them control of deception for
all operations. In the past, when a naval commander got Chiefs
of Staff approval for an operation, either N.I.D. (in other words
17M) and the Twenty Committee took over the deception if the
operation was completely naval, or the Inter Service Security
Board and the Twenty Committee (which included 17M) carried
it out if there were other Services involved. In the early stages
of the L.C.S. the Chiefs of Staff made a request direct to the
L.C.S. that they should provide deception, and on more than
one occasion they provided a plan without any contact with
N.I.D. Uncle John was then suddenly faced with a deception
plan, sometimes long and complicated, and a request for his
observations 'immediately'.

Fortunately J.C. had little difficulty in persuading Johnny
Bevan of the potential usefulness to him of B.1A's agents, and
of the readiness of everyone to co-operate, and I had the chance
to show that that was also my attitude. Although 'C' had, somewhat belatedly, agreed to provide Johnny Bevan with such of
Special Intelligence as might help him, it was soon apparent that

this information was only passed very slowly, and even then not all that he needed was passed. I got Uncle John's permission to pass what I thought might help, which I could do more quickly, and with greater knowledge of what Johnny Bevan needed, than apparently could the officer deputed by 'C' to carry out the duty. This was in breach of the arrangement with 'C' limiting the people to whom I could pass Special Intelligence, but Uncle John never paid attention to such things if they hindered the war effort. And the proof of the pudding was in the eating; as events showed, he never made a mistake – or certainly not one of this kind, only the minor one of lack of tact that brought about his downfall.

In any case, this arrangement did not have to last long, as the material soon started to come through properly from 'C', but it did give me the chance to show that I also wanted to co-operate. So everyone got down to working together well and the L.C.S. rapidly gained expertise, so much so that they were able to organize and co-ordinate the wholly successful and invaluable cover for Overlord.

There were, however, at least two occasions when the new inflexible system, requiring reference to the Chiefs of Staff, resulted in a veto on promising deception plans, though to be fair one of the plans would probably have had to go to them anyway.

That was a proposal of mine. The Russians were under great pressure, to say the least, and were urging a second front in Europe. We could not yet give them one, but could we do anything which might draw some weight off them? I knew that the Germans were very worried about an attack in the Bay of Biscay area. That was absolutely certain from frequent messages in Special Intelligence – Abwehr messages, Army messages, Luftwaffe messages, High Command appreciations. There were discussions among the Germans whether all efforts should be concentrated on reinforcing the defences on the Channel coast or whether some, and if so how much, should be spared for the Biscay coast, and whether the troops there were not too thin on the ground.

To foster that belief could both lessen the material and weapons available for Channel coast defences and *might* divert some troops from being sent to the Russian front. We could easily have done this.

But the plan had to go to the Chiefs of Staff and they turned it down flat on the grounds that an attack on the Biscay coast was so impossible that the deception would be incredible. With great respect, that last point usurped our function – *we* were the experts on deception, *they* were wholly ignorant about this art. If they thought, as they apparently did, that the deception would be useful, it was for us to decide whether we could put it over.

Their reason was that *they* knew that the Biscay coast was outside the range of our fighter aircraft, so the necessary cover could not be given for a prolonged invasion, and *they* knew that we hadn't got enough aircraft carriers to spare to give fighter cover even for an 'in and out' operation of real magnitude – all of which was of course quite correct. But they couldn't make themselves *think as Germans*. The Germans did not know what our Chiefs of Staff did and, on *their* information, they *did* think that we had enough forces and material for us to risk at least a major in and out operation under Russian pressure.

It was so important to deception work to be able to put oneself completely in the mind of the enemy, to think as *they* would think on *their* information and decide what *they* would do – ignoring what you knew yourself and what you could do. As an illustration, our experts alleged that Field-Marshal Jödl showed strange ignorance of the requirements for an amphibious assault, when he later stated that an invasion was expected in the South of France in March or April 1944, as in fact there were not sufficient Allied ships, assault craft or troops in that area. The experts did not know that Jödl had plenty of reports of quite enough ships, assault craft *and* troops being there. These mainly came from free-lance agents in North Africa who worked on the basis that the more that they reported, the better pay they got.

Those experts did not possess the facts to get the right answer – but we had given the Chiefs of Staff the facts about the Bay of Biscay Operation and they ought to have done better. But perhaps I am being unfair to them. Service training is not the same as that of a barrister. We have to learn throughout our career to put ourselves in our opponents' place and try to anticipate what he will think and what he will do on *his* information. Maybe that is why I so regretted not being allowed to try out my idea about Bay of Biscay landings.

The second plan frustrated in this way was not very important in itself and was not actually a double agent plan. Before Plan Fortitude, the huge deception plan to cover Overlord, could get fully under way the policy was to try to get the Germans to think that we might delay our invasion across the Channel as long as possible, in the hope of avoiding it altogether as the Germans would be brought to their knees by our bombing.

The plan was as follows. Some German officers, including a general, were due to be repatriated under the Geneva Convention. A British general who knew this German general from before the war, should visit him in the prison camp. He should lead the conversation round and say that it was frightful that the war should go on with so much loss of life, ruining two great nations. Were the Germans continuing because they thought we were going to invade and they would throw us back into the sea? We weren't such fools. We weren't going to lose all our young men like in the last war. Of course we were making preparations on our South Coast but this was partly a bluff to keep the Russians happy and partly to be ready to march in when Germany was crushed by our bombing. He didn't mind speaking frankly as there was nothing that the Germans could do about it, and he hoped that the Germans, a once great nation, would not commit suicide.

We knew that the German general concerned was receptive to such talk and the scheme could surely do no harm, even if it only succeeded to the extent of causing a bit of dissension in the German General Staff, some of whom were, as we knew also, against continuing the slaughter, as the bomb plot at Hitler's H.Q. was later to show. And we had the right British general who was willing to play.

The plan had to go to the Chiefs of Staff under the new inflexible procedure. For some reason they decided that the Foreign Office must be consulted and, this time, the Prime Minister as well. The Foreign Office did not object. Unfortunately Winston

Churchill was away. The Deputy Prime Minister vetoed the plan, giving as his reason that 'it would be prejudicial to the Chief of the Imperial General Staff'. What on earth did he mean? No one has ever explained.

13

Operation Mincemeat

In the summer of 1942, while Operation Torch, the landing in North Africa, was being mounted, the Twenty Committee had to plan ahead. When it came to questions of strategy the German High Command needed no lessons from us. If the next target was clear to us it must also be clear to them. How could we possibly mislead them?

The problem arose from the shape of the Mediterranean. Many people think of it as an oval expanse of water. It is, in fact, shaped like an hour glass. It is pinched into a narrow waist by the point of Tunisia to the south and the toe of Italy, together with Sicily, to the north. It was for this reason and because of the continuous attacks by land-based aircraft from Sicily that convoys to Malta were so terribly costly.

Against that background the next step by the Allies was obvious. As Churchill was to say later, 'Everyone but a bloody fool would *know* that it's Shishily.'*

It was decided that we could not hope to persuade the Germans that we were not going to attack Sicily at all, but we *might* persuade them that we would try to surprise them by capturing Sardinia first and then come down to Sicily afterwards, from the

* This conversation with Churchill is the only thing wrongly recorded in my book *The Man Who Never Was*; in 1952 the Prime Minister's secretariat insisted that a Prime Minister could not be recorded as having said 'bloody' and insisted on its being altered to 'damned'. Today we are more realistic and permissive!

north. And, if we were very successful, we *might* get even the professional German High Command to believe that we were going to be rash enough both to try that and begin a Balkan invasion almost simultaneously. They did not know how short we were of shipping, landing-craft etc., partly because our double agents had been exaggerating our rate of building of vessels of both kinds in their reports.

At several meetings that summer the Twenty Committee had puzzled what, if anything, could usefully be done to deceive the Germans. No agent's reports could hope to cause the German High Command to alter the strategic measures that it planned with Sicily such an obvious target. Something as material as a document which was obviously 'genuine' might answer, however. But, even if we could devise such a document, how could we get it to them? And then, all of a sudden, a scheme emerged.

While I was puzzling over how to 'cover' Sicily, the penny suddenly dropped. Why not get a really top-level personal letter, signed by one general and addressed to another general serving in North Africa, conveying the information that we were not going to invade Sicily only by 'reading between the lines' but nevertheless absolutely clearly. We would then 'plant' it on to a dead body dressed as an officer who was, as often happened although against regulations, carrying it to give personally to the addressee. Such a body need not be dropped but could be placed in the sea where it would float ashore in Spain. We knew from Special Intelligence of several places in that country where any papers found on the body would be virtually certain to be given to the Germans. The actual placing of the body in the sea might be done by flying boat, an escorting warship which diverged from its convoy along the coast of Spain, or a submarine. It could be made to appear as if the body had come from an aircraft which had had to ditch in the sea while flying out to Algiers, as many would be doing at that time.

The Twenty Committee approved the idea and, in due course, Charles Cholmondeley, one of two R.A.F. representatives concerned, and I, were given the job of getting everything ready to 'go'. J.C. had wisely foreseen that even when all was ready for the actual operation to start it would be difficult to persuade the

Chiefs of Staff that it was worth trying. If we were to seek authority earlier they would find a thousand reasons why it would be impossible to concoct a letter and prepare a body which would have the remotest chance of deceiving the Germans. The only hope was to provide them with everything ready and completely convincing.

Charles and I worked very happily together, always thinking on the same lines and easily resolving any differences of opinion. Each of us carried out the parts of the job which he could do best.

There were three vital problems. Could we get a suitable body? Could we concoct a letter or other document which could plausibly be carried by an officer in an aircraft going to Algiers and convince the Germans that Sicily was not our next target? Could we manufacture documents which would make it plausible that our officer was carrying such a document?

We searched and searched for a body. There were, sadly enough, plenty of dead bodies in London and elsewhere but most had died from causes which were plainly discernible and inconsistent with death after an aircraft had ditched in the sea. An even more difficult factor was that almost every body belongs to somebody – to relatives who would naturally be reluctant to allow it to be taken away and used for some secret purpose, whatever we might say vaguely about the national importance of that purpose. The question of security arose here too. We nearly gave up in despair before clearing the first fence.

Then suddenly, with the help of Bentley Purchase, a well-known coroner, we found the perfect body. I gave a solemn promise never to reveal whose body it was and, as there is no one alive from whom I can get a release, I can say no more than that it was the body of a young man who had died of pneumonia. As I am not identifying him, I can perhaps add the ironic fact that he was a bit of a ne'er-do-well, and that the only worthwhile thing that he ever did he did after his death – and how worthwhile that was! I'm sure that it made up for everything else.

Next I had to consult the great pathologist, Sir Bernard Spilsbury, whom I had known in peace time. Not only was he brilliant at his job but he was closer to being an 'oyster' than anyone else that I have ever known, not only absolutely secure from temptation to gossip but also completely incurious about any facet of a problem that did not concern him. When I had told him that we wanted to float a body on to a foreign coast, wearing a Mae West lifejacket as if it had come from a ditched aircraft, he never asked me why or any other question except one that he *had* to ask if he was to give me an accurate answer. 'Into what country?' I told him Spain, and he gave his verdict. This I can summarise as 'Oh that's all right. Although such a man would almost certainly die of exposure rather than drowning, he would swallow a good deal of water. There will be pleural fluid in the lungs of *your* body and to detect that it wasn't sea-water would take as good and careful a pathologist as I am – and they haven't got one in Spain.' He was never a modest man but he was seldom wrong!

He advised us to keep the body frozen in a mortuary until we needed to use it and then to pack it in an air-tight container full of 'dry-ice' – not in a hopeless attempt to keep it frozen but so as to exclude oxygen which is the main cause of decomposition.

Next there was the 'deception' letter. An excellent one was written by General Sir Archibald Nye, the Vice-Chief of the Imperial General Staff, after I had discussed the requirements with him. Obviously such a letter could not be an official one dealing with the Allied plans as that would go in a self-destructive or self-sinking bag. It had to be a letter between two friends, on topics that the writer would not want to be seen by the recipient's deputy, so that it might plausibly go by the hand of an officer. Then at one stage the letter could 'carelessly' give away the Allied plans and show that we were not going to invade Sicily. Sir Archibald, once he had appreciated those requirements, composed a quite brilliant letter to Alexander who commanded the British forces in North-West Africa under Eisenhower. In it he explained 'off the record' why Eisenhower's request for the Dodecanese as the cover, or deception, target for his invasion across the Mediterranean could not be granted by the Chiefs of Staff, in spite of the desirability of having a cover target as far from the real target as possible. The Dodecanese had been approved as the cover target for the operation from

Egypt. He added *en passant*, that General Wilson, in Egypt, would have a difficult task as there were reports that the Germans were adding to their forces in Greece so we were increasing our troops assaulting two named places. Eisenhower would have to put up with Sicily as his cover target. Finally, he gave his reasons for our decision in a friendly dispute with the Americans about decorations for the troops when British were serving alongside Americans.

This letter could not have been bettered. Quite casually, in a letter between friends written to dispel misunderstanding which might arise, he gave away Greece as an objective of an invasion from Egypt, and Sicily as the *cover* target in the West. This had the added advantage that, if the Germans heard an accurate 'leak' about an invasion of Sicily, they might merely think that that was a part of our deception. And the last bit, about the medals, afforded an added reason why the letter should not go through normal channels lest it should be read by Alexander's American deputy, in the integrated H.Q., if Alexander was away for some reason.

Before getting down to a solution of the third, the crucial, question we had to give our body a name and a rank. We had thought of him as a soldier, simply because there were so many more of them than officers of the other Services. But we found a snag straight away. The War Office system of signal distribution was such that, if the body of an officer was reported as having been washed ashore in Spain, the signals would be distributed to anyone in the War Office or elsewhere who might be even remotely concerned and it would soon be discovered that no such officer really existed. And there was no way of limiting such a distribution of signals without arousing even more talk.

This had surprised me as in the Admiralty a request on the authority of the Director of Naval Intelligence to the War Registry that any signals on a particular subject should be sent to Lieutenant-Commander Montagu (or some other named person) only was not unusual and would be carried out without either surprise or comment. So we thought we would make him a naval officer until we realized that they didn't wear battle-dress at that time of the war but uniforms that fitted and we couldn't take our corpse to Gieves to have him measured and fitted! So he had to become a Royal Marine. And we chose the name of William Martin because there was a group of several officers of that name, including a W.R.N. Martin, of about the right seniority for his age in the current public Navy List. Therefore the probability was that if the Germans had access to a Navy List the thing would remain plausible and if any friend of one of the Martins (in, say, Gibraltar) heard of the death they would merely think that the initials had become confused.

The solution of the third crucial question was made much easier by the ready help that we got from Lord Louis Mountbatten who, at that time, was Chief of Combined Operations. Our body became that of Major Martin, Royal Marines, an expert on Tank Landing Craft, who was going to Algiers to help to iron out some problems that they were notionally having out there. He carried another excellent letter, signed by Lord Louis, which 'gave away' that fact and asked Admiral Sir Andrew Cunningham, the Commander-in-Chief Mediterranean, to ensure that the letter that Major Martin carried reached General Alexander safely as it was highly personal.

This letter included some little pointers to keep on directing the German deductions on to the right road. It ended 'let me have him back please as soon as the assault is over. He might bring some sardines with him – they are on points* here!' Lord Louis recognized that that was but a poor joke, but he readily included it – appreciating, as few others did, that it was to the Germans and to *their* sense of humour, and not to ours, that it was directed. As we learnt later, the Germans *did* pick on that joke as confirming their deductions from the rest of our deception that the next Allied target was Sardinia.

Lord Louis included a sentence describing how good Major Martin really was at his job – a sentence to the effect that he had been right on some points about the Dieppe raid when the rest of those at Combined Operations H.Q. had been wrong. I wanted that sentence in as I felt sure that no German agent could resist sending on to Berlin a full copy of a letter, even a letter only of introduction and request, in which the Chief of Com-

* i.e. on the supplementary rationing.

bined Operations seemed to admit that the Dieppe raid was a
failure – and I wanted the whole letter with the joke about
Sardinia to go on. Sure enough, as it turned out, the only documents of which full copies, rather than summaries, went on to
Berlin were Sir Archibald Nye's letter and this chatty letter of
introduction. So the bait was swallowed.

We had now got the document which would convey the official side of Major Martin's personality to the Germans, and the
reason why he was making the journey and carrying the deception letter. However, we felt that it was necessary to 'make him
a human being' as that would be much more convincing than if
he remained just the body of an officer. Again this could only be
done by the documents which he carried – so we let him notionally get engaged so that he could plausibly carry letters that
made him into a real person, and we provided him with letters
and a photo from his fiancée, letters from his father and others
consequent on his forthcoming marriage, bills and so on.

We even made sure that the fingerprints on such documents
as would 'take' prints were only those which would normally
be there; mine were used for Major Martin's throughout – he
would be safely buried before anyone could start checking his
fingerprints.

I also had to arrange for Major Martin's transport. Admiral
Sir Claud Barry, the Flag Officer, Submarines, arranged to alter
the sailing date of H.M. submarine *Seraph*, commanded by the
then Lieutenant-Commander Jewell, to suit our proposed time-
table.

I had had the task, as a mere Lieutenant-Commander
R.N.V.R., of persuading all these very senior officers to co-
operate in all this in spite of my having to tell them that the
whole thing was subject to approval by the Chiefs of Staff, which
we had not yet asked for and might not get. And all this was at
a time when deception was not widely known – to say the least.
It is yet another sign of the great quality of these officers that
this proved to be almost the easiest part of the whole operation.

Then the complete plan went through the London Controlling
Section to the Chiefs of Staff who passed the buck yet again and

insisted that the plan should be submitted to the Prime Minister. *He* had no qualms – it was the kind of thing he enjoyed.

So in April 1943 we had to get the body out of cold storage at the mortuary where it had been since November 1942 and take it in a canister that Charles had had designed and specially made, up to the Clyde where it was delivered to *Seraph* lying in the Holy Loch. There I gave to Jewell some informal 'operation orders' and advice before he sailed to Huelva off which port he launched the body in a Mae West life-jacket, taking the all-important documents with it.

The Spanish and Germans in Huelva and Madrid played their parts as we had relied on them to do. The papers were shown to the Germans in Madrid by the Spaniards, who then lied to us officially as I had known that they would do. Then copies were sent on to the Abwehr in Berlin; they in turn passed them to the German High Command and to Hitler himself. These also swallowed our deception whole. Troops were sent to Sardinia and Corsica and the defences of those islands were strengthened, both at the expense of Sicily – and even there the defences of the north coast were increased at the expense of those on the south coast where we landed. In addition, as the V.C.I.G.S.'s letter had indicated simultaneous landings in Greece as well as in Sardinia, Rommel was sent to command the defences of that country, a Panzer Division was sent right across Europe from France to the road junction covering the two places mentioned in the letter, minefields were laid off the coast and German motor-torpedo boats were sent from Sicily to the Aegean. As General Lord Ismay, the Prime Minister's Chief of Staff, said in the foreword to my book, we had 'spread-eagled the German defensive effort right across Europe.'

I doubt whether any 'crime' has ever been more meticulously prepared – for it was in essence a large-scale fraud. Indeed, my first excursion into crime gave me an understanding of how fascinating a criminal's life can be, and why some men and women prefer it to any other and, in spite of what some theoreticians may contend, do not want to be reformed.

14

Overlord - The Invasion of France

There was a relaxation in the tempo of strategic deception through double agents after Torch in North Africa in 1942, because Operation Mincemeat for Husky in Sicily was carried out by other means. This period was mainly filled with what we used to call *ad hoc* deceptions, some of which I have instanced. 17M was busier than ever with the Orange Summaries and the Abwehr messages, besides numerous miscellaneous jobs. On top of this was the almost daily task of providing and checking 'chicken-feed' for the agents to pass on naval matters, always aiming at our ultimate objective, cover and deception for Overlord. For that purpose we *had* to build up the agents' credibility and accuracy in the eyes of the Germans so that they would come to rely on them, and would discredit any other casual information, any leak or even fairly regular reports from neutral diplomats.

A plan, eventually code-named Fortitude, was worked out to take advantage of the ever-continuing low-level leakage, and here came the justification for the setting-up of the London Controlling Section with its direct access to, and complete liaison with, first the planners of Overlord and then the Supreme Commander's Intelligence Staff. Eisenhower, with his great talent for inter-Allied co-operation and the avoidance of those inter-Allied jealousies which caused so much harm in the 1914–18 war, recognized that the British had far more experience in deception than did the Americans and wisely decided to leave it to us, merely appointing a few officers to liaise with L.C.S.

The target for the approved plan was simple to define. No one could prevent the Germans knowing that an invasion was coming in 1944. Considering the weather pattern, even the time of crossing the Channel and starting a tank campaign in France could be closely anticipated. The one real hope was to prevent them knowing where we intended to land. The Germans, as we knew from the Special Intelligence intercepts of Hitler's messages and those of the German High Command and their Commanders in France, corroborated by all sorts of informal but lower level messages, considered that the Allied invasion might take place anywhere along the coast from Normandy through the Pas de Calais. They considered the latter rather more likely, especially because of the short sea passage and the resultant possibility of our providing much more land-based fighter-cover for the landings.

On the other hand they knew that we knew how strong their defences were on the Pas de Calais coast and reasoned that we might accept the disadvantage of the wider sea crossing to Normandy, in the hope that the defences, and especially the strength of the German forces and reserves, would be less in that area.

The objective given to the L.C.S. was therefore twofold. Basically, to accept that the Germans would know when the invasion would come to within a very short period, but to try to prevent their knowing the exact day – this could only be done by security means and no deception could work. There were also lesser deception targets for the South of France operations, but I do not propose to describe them in this story of 'my war' as I took little part in them. They broadly followed the pattern of the main deceptions.

The task given to the deceptioneers was concerned mainly with the most important and most difficult of those objectives – to try to get the Germans to act on the belief that our attack would take place in the Pas de Calais. If we could not succeed in that, we must try to get them to believe, and to act on the belief, that the main attack would take place there and that any other attacks were diversions. In the event we succeeded in getting the best of both worlds, first the one effect and then the other.

Of course the agents could not have succeeded without what was called physical deception, but no success at all could have been achieved without the agents.

Colonel Bevan had the whole authority of the Chiefs of Staff behind his L.C.S., and they did a magnificent job with dummy ships and dummy camps, backed by bogus wireless traffic as the Germans were monitoring this by High Frequency Direction Finding. This was our old friend Huffduff, which we also had been using since the start of the war to back up Special Intelligence and give us something during any barren period when the Germans had changed a cipher and we had not yet broken the new one.

Most of these bogus activities were based on the East Coast and Kent so as to shift the impression that the Germans gained of the weight of our preparations as far to the north and east as possible.

In the early planning period there were not enough signallers available to create the right impression, so various agents gave indications of preparations being made, such as construction of camps and so on. Later the agents' reports, made credible to the Germans by the growing signal traffic on the air, created a completely false order of battle. The rest of the physical deception was handicapped by the infrequency of German reconnaissance flights.

This deception was worked as follows. We would have in notional existence during the run up to D-day two complete army groups, one real (21st Army Group) and one notional (First U.S. Army Group, FUSAG). Then, after the real 21st Army Group landed in Normandy it would leave the notional FUSAG behind in eastern England. This would consist of two large completely non-existent Army Groups, the 14th U.S. Army and the 4th British Army, thus maintaining the threat on the Pas de Calais, even after the D-day landings. This situation had been made possible by our agents having created a notional situation, during the build-up period, that our troops were mainly in the south-east and east of England and in Scotland instead of in their actual positions in the midlands, south-west and west of England. The way the deception was worked, backed by the physical deception, was by a mass of sighting reports made by a number of agents, mostly Garbo's sub-agents; these reported divisional signs of vehicles, uniforms and so on, and were backed by notional higher-level 'leaks' reported by other agents.

These false agents' reports were highly successful. In Italy our forces captured a German map showing the Allied 'order of battle' on 15 May 1944, about three weeks before D-day. This was based mainly on reports from sub-agents of the Garbo network and those of another agent, Brutus. Their locations and identifications of troops were virtually as they had been fed to them. Then we captured in France a recognition booklet, which had been issued to commanders in the field, which included coloured illustrations of all our completely notional divisional signs among those of the real divisions.

Sighting reports and other instances of what might be called ordinary spying were backed up by other deceptions. One example will suffice to show how a very peripheral report may be useful as back-up. A double agent whom we called Mullett had been fairly high-up in the insurance world in Belgium with a company which had a good deal of business insuring buildings in northern France; the task which he had been set by the Germans was more to find out about our production and economics than about military matters, and his cover-job in England was a business one, which fitted in well with the message we now got him to send. This was that an English Government Department, which knew that he had a very great deal of information about industries, buildings and so on in northern France, had asked him to supply as much of that as he could *about the area of Calais* as an urgent matter. An additional bonus was that he reported to Brussels, and the Abwehr seemed to be extra impressed about reports that were 'pointers' from which inferences could be drawn, if they received pointers from a number of different out-stations, all pointing in the same direction, rather than from one out-station.

As all the world knows, on D-day, 6 June 1944, our troops landed not in the Pas de Calais but in Normandy. That this was a surprise was confirmed at the time by Special Intelligence. We had done all that was expected of us – but there was in fact a bonus. Now for the second stage of the deception plan we tried to keep the Germans convinced, for as long as possible, that the Normandy landings were a large-scale diversion to draw German forces away from the Pas de Calais where the real invasion would be made by our notional army.

We were much more favourably placed than we had anticipated, as we had convinced the Germans more definitely than we could have hoped. We got evidence of this when Special Intelligence threw up a message from the Japanese military attaché in Berlin to his colleagues in other European capitals that it was still expected that there would be an invasion shortly in the area of Calais and Dunkirk as 'one separate Army Group is still stationed in the south-east of England.' This message was sent out on June 9 and apparently was based on an interview with his contact in the High Command on the evening before – and the 8th was two days *after* D-day!

Our agents continued to report that the troops were still in the east and south-east of England, though showing even more of those signs of activity which presaged something happening very shortly. They were backed up by reports of some notional movements of shipping and, of course, by sustained bogus wireless traffic.

We do not know whether we were responsible for what then happened. Much of the possible German reinforcements which could have gone to Normandy were kept in position to support the front-line troops in the Pas de Calais area for the first vital ten days. By the time that the Germans did decide to move them, Allied bombing and the French resistance movement had had time to do so much damage to the railway lines that their arrival in Normandy was still further delayed.

When the post-mortem was made on Overlord and Fortitude the Chiefs of Staff had no hesitation in deciding that the work of double agents had been an invaluable success. Indeed in December 1944 Garbo was awarded the M.B.E. for the services that he had rendered to this country. It is fascinating that the Germans were equally satisfied with his work in sending the

completely bogus reports about Overlord and had, in June 1944,
awarded him the Iron Cross – a most exceptional award as they
had to give him, a Spaniard, special naturalization as a German
in order to do it. I doubt whether anyone else has ever been
decorated by both sides for the same messages!

There can be no doubt that the contribution of the double
agents to the success of the Overlord landings and to the initial
successes of the campaign for the liberation of France was immense.

15

V-bombs

When the Allies were fighting their way across France our main objective on the strategic side of deception had been accomplished. The Twenty Committee throughout had placed in the forefront of their aims the preservation and build-up of agents so that they could play their part in protecting the landings in France – gaining as many other advantages as possible meanwhile without risking the compromising of any really worthwhile agent.

Now we had to take stock of our position. Could the Germans really believe in our agents any longer after the Pas de Calais had not been attacked from the sea? Some of us thought that they must be blown, which would make their use for any further deception unacceptably dangerous and, in any case, little could arise on the strategic side in which they could help. Fortunately the majority of us strongly believed that we should continue and see what happened – the best of the agents, at least, might not be blown because the reports that they put over had been so well designed that there was a real hope that the Germans would conclude that the agents had been right all along – that the Allies *had* been going to cross to the Pas de Calais after drawing German troops to Normandy to resist a diversionary attack there, and that, when the Germans did not move their troops, and the diversionary landings had been 'unexpectedly' successful, we had altered our plans. Had something like that happened we could at least hope to put over very useful ad hoc deceptions. I argued strongly for that last factor as it was the Navy, partly due to its different situation, which had done most of this type of double-cross work. Eventually we were virtually unanimously in favour of carrying on, especially as we all agreed that there was no knowing what was going to turn up in this war.

But it was V-weapons that now occupied our main attention. We already knew a good deal about V-bombs, having had the first warnings and a reasonable amount of detail from Special Intelligence. In early May 1944 Tricycle gained us useful warning that the bombs were coming soon. He lived and worked in London and the Germans valued him so highly that they sent him a message advising him to move out of London as quickly as he could as that town would soon be blasted by Hitler's secret weapons.

This imminent new form of attack had reinforced the arguments that the future *might* bring circumstances in which we could gain entirely unforeseen advantages from our double agents, *if* the Germans still believed their reports. But almost at once we were faced with a desperate problem.

As soon as the bombs started to fall, the Germans ordered all the agents in the London area to report the time and place of explosions together with the damage done, and to do it as quickly as possible. If the agents were to be kept 'alive', there was no possible way in which they could avoid obeying these orders. Not only did the newspapers identify many of the places hit, often with maps, but the agents could not help seeing them. How could they fail to report a V-1 falling in, let us say, Piccadilly when all the Spanish Embassy must have known that one had done so? So what were our agents to say in their messages?

We *had* to make a decision, and do it *fast*. Fortunately the representative of the Home Defence Executive on the Twenty Committee was John Drew, a most able civil servant with a really fertile imagination and great ingenuity. Also, fortunately, the H.D.E. member of the W-Board was Sir Findlater Stewart (one of the rare holders of a 'Double G', a G.C.B. and a G.C.I.E.) who was soon to show the quality that justified the distinction.

The plan was brilliant in its conception and in its simplicity. It was immediately apparent that bombs near the centre of

London, which was densely populated and full of workers in day-time when many of the bombs fell, caused far more casualties and did far more damage to buildings essential to the war effort than did bombs which fell further to the south or east. The plan was therefore to report as many bombs as the agents would be likely to see in their notional employments or activities or to learn about, but to give wrong times of impact. If a bomb fell in the central area of London agents should report that it fell at the time when a bomb fell between five and ten miles short. This, it was considered, would cause the Germans to believe that the shorter range-setting was the right one.

Obviously this was not a scheme which the W-Board could authorize on its own responsibility, nor was it within L.C.S.'s charter of responsibility for deception in connection with operations. So it was put up to the Chiefs of Staff for submission to the War Cabinet. The Chiefs backed it on the realistic basis that the V-1s which were not shot down were bound to fall somewhere, and it was better that they should fall where they would cause the least casualties and damage. Unfortunately Churchill was away again at a conference and the decision was based on the cowardly principle that no one was entitled to decide that A should die rather than B, and the scheme was vetoed.

At this point Sir Findlater Stewart revealed his great courage. After his briefing by John Drew he was convinced that the Germans valued several of our agents highly and would accept their reports even to the extent that if, say, a Spanish diplomat bothered to give the time of the fall of a bomb which differed from the double agent's report, the Germans would accept the agent's time and decide that the diplomat had got the time wrong. This would suffice to govern the Germans' range setting.

Even more important, he was convinced that when Winston Churchill returned he would withdraw the veto. But we couldn't wait. The agents' reports *had* to be sent now or never. So Sir Findlater, backed by Duncan Sandys, the Minister in charge of anti-V-bomb measures, had the great courage to tell us to go ahead.

Churchill returned and the scheme was re-submitted – slightly

altered for form's sake thought not in any material particular –
and Sir Findlater was proved right as the decision was that we
should go ahead – although for political reasons, our mandate
was phrased very vaguely.

I took no part in the carrying out of this operation in which
the case-officers of B.1A worked wonders, with well-devised reports, and so co-ordinated a mass of messages as to avoid any
really crossed lines, but also introduced enough slight differences
in the times reported to produce a total picture that seemed real.

As we plotted the real mean point of impact (M.P.I.) of the
V–1s and our phoney M.P.I. we were thrilled to see that the real
one seemed to draw back steadily, as we intended it to do. Indeed, in one period of four weeks at the beginning of 1945 it
drew back about two miles a week and ended up well outside
the London region, with the bombs mostly falling in sparsely
populated areas. That this was due to the agents' reports was
indicated by the fact that, when the launching sites were moved
up the enemy coast as our troops advanced, the M.P.I. moved
nearer the centre of London again, and then once more moved
back. When V–2s started to fall, exactly the same thing happened
and the M.P.I. was steadily moved back from the centre of
London.

After the war we received confirmation of our success. Among
captured documents we found a map which the Germans had
used to make a plot of the fall of the V-bombs over two weeks.
We found that it was based on our agents' reports, and that the
M.P.I. was centred near Charing Cross, when the bombs had been
falling in much less densely populated areas. The operation had
worked!

That the operation was justified was also checked in a different
way – and quite independently by an expert who had no knowledge of our work and believed that, if there were any aiming or
range errors, they were solely due to German miscalculations.
The expert had made a calculation of what difference it would
have made in casualties alone if the M.P.I. each week had been
five miles further west than it in fact was during the period when
the rockets were fired more nearly from east to west after the
Allied advance had caused the Germans to relocate their firing

sites. The calculations showed that if the rocket-bombs had been 'properly ranged' even that much further forward, many thousands more people would have lost their lives during the bombardment.

The country has good cause to thank the agents, and Sir Findlater Stewart.

F

16

Work and Outside Life, 1942-1945

In early October 1942, D.N.I.'s secretary told me that Uncle John had started a docket suggesting that I should be promoted; he had written that my duties were so secret that he could not specify them but they carried great responsibility. He added that I also represented him on a number of committees on which my opposite numbers from the other Services were of much higher rank. They were, in fact, a Brigadier, two full Colonels, one Group-Captain, two Wing-Commanders and a Lieutenant-Colonel. However, a bit later on, the secretary told me that the recommendation had been turned down flat as, once again, I was not in the Special Branch but in the Executive Branch with no sea-time. This was depressing. Not only would scrambled eggs on one's cap be nice for my ego, but the increase of pay would have lessened the anxiety of my forbearing bank manager.

When I had learnt of this veto I went down to our subterranean dungeon and there worked out my anger and disappointment by composing a personal submission to the Second Sea Lord.

It read:

1. It is requested that I may be given permission to relinquish my commission in the R.N.V.R. in order to be free to join the German Navy.
2. The reason for this request is that my services are appreciated more highly by Admiral Canaris than they appear to be by Their Lordships. The former has just awarded me a

special bonus and had agreed to my pay being increased.

(Sgd.) Ewen E. S. Montagu

Failed-Commander, R.N.V.R.

Such a submission seemed to me to be fully justified by the fact that Admiral Canaris *had* just done that for one of Tate's notional sub-agents in appreciation of a very high-level (though wholly untruthful) report that I had just sent through him. But, naturally, the submission to the Second Sea Lord was *not* sent!

It was only much later, not long before VE-day, that I learnt the other, the main, reason for the refusal. I happened to be waiting to go in to see the First Sea Lord when his secretary, Captain (S.) 'Tim' Shaw, expressed surprise that I hadn't ever got the other half-stripe, and asked me whether I knew why. I said that Uncle John had recommended it twice, but it had been turned down because I had no sea-time, and that I believed that Admiral Rushbrooke, Uncle John's successor after his reposting, had also done it once with no better result. Tim Shaw asked me whether, if it would help, I would be willing to join the Green Line (the slang description of the Special Branch who had a green backing between their gold stripes). I told him that I took pride in being in 'the real R.N.V.R.' having joined to go to sea, and it wasn't worth changing, especially at that late stage in the war. Then I went in to talk to the First Sea Lord.

A few days later I was in Tim Shaw's room, again waiting, when he told me that he had sent for the dockets in case anything could be done. Apparently the Second Sea Lord, who deals with personnel, had replied to Uncle John that, unless he knew what I was doing, he wouldn't sanction my promotion. When the docket returned to Uncle John it must have found him in one of his worst moods, excusable considering the burden that he was carrying. His answer was that the essence of security was 'need to know' and that my work was far too secret for the Second Sea Lord to know about – and he didn't need to know as he should accept that it merited promotion for me on the word of the Director of Naval Intelligence. Tim Shaw added, 'I can't tell you what the reply from the Second Sea Lord was – but I *can* tell you that it would effectively bar your ever getting promotion if you were Nelson himself.' So I eventually finished the war still a Lieutenant-Commander.

In November 1942 we got our first inkling that Uncle John was to leave us. He had always handled everyone tactlessly, but this time it was apparently the high-ups whom he had treated roughly, and several of his colleagues on the Joint Intelligence Committee promptly took the opportunity of plunging their knives into his back. He was to be 'promoted' to Flag Officer Commanding, Royal Indian Navy, and he was to leave us. Everyone in N.I.D., even those of us who had suffered most from his methods, regarded it as a real tragedy. He was a truly *great* intelligence officer.

Just before he went, he rang down on the phone for me to come to his room. There he told me that he was going to confide in me about something, and I must regard it as even more secret than even the super-secrecy of Special Intelligence and double-cross. He then told me of the atom bomb, code-named Manhattan Project, and the places where the research and experiments were going on. He confided in me because if the Germans ever got an inkling of what we were doing, it would probably emerge in our Special Intelligence, particularly the Abwehr traffic, or in questions to double agents. He had noticed, from one of my verbal reports to him, that one of the instructions given to Tricycle in addition to his high level questionnaire when he went to America, was to report if he could on production of uranium, and anything else about that substance. Tricycle at that time was probably our highest-level general-information agent and it might even be significant that no other agent had yet been asked any questions which could link with atomic research. Uncle John had been acting as long-stop and had asked me questions from time to time, the purpose of which was naturally unknown to me. He would no longer be able to do so, and felt it was essential that I should know what I must be on the look-out for. Probably no one else, even outside N.I.D., had the same wide and detailed daily coverage of both Special Intelligence and double agent traffic that I had. Now that I was aware of Manhattan Project I would be the first to spot, probably in a quite irrelevant message, if the Germans were getting warmer.

I had two rather different surprises after he had gone. In the Navy, with a change of commanding officer you get a sort of character reference, always known as a flimsy from the paper of the form used. Generally these vary only in the epithet, if any, inserted in between the words 'to my ... satisfaction'. Infrequently a commendation is added, and, to my surprise, Uncle John added a longish tribute including 'the unique attainments of this officer have been of the greatest value to the Navy.' The second even greater surprise came when I received a very charming personal letter of thanks from him. Looking back, it may be that he judged that he got the best out of me by rough, icy, unsympathetic treatment.

Uncle John was succeeded by Commodore Rushbrooke. He was not a fit man. He had had an exhausting war culminating in his aircraft carrier being torpedoed. I am sure that he would have himself agreed that intelligence work was not really his bent and that he would rather have had any other appointment. The N.I.D. view was that the high-ups, tired of being bullied by Uncle John, were deliberately opting for less rough treatment and felt that Uncle John had got N.I.D. to such a peak of efficiency that it could freewheel until the war ended. However, though we never ceased to miss Uncle John, our admiration for the way Commodore (later Rear Admiral) Rushbrooke coped with a task in which he can never really have been happy grew steadily.

It was at this time, early in 1943, that Iris suggested that she and the family should come back to England. She was enjoying her job with Security Co-ordination and her apartment in New York but felt strongly that Jeremy, in particular, would miss a great deal, and be estranged from most of his generation, if he had not experienced England in war-time and had not been to an English school. After all, he was over fifteen by now.

This put me in a quandary. Much though I longed to have them back, I knew that Iris's belief (that the bombing danger – like the danger of invasion – was at an end) was wrong. I knew of the V-bombs still probably to come. No one yet could assess what that bombardment would be like. But, of course I could not tell her. The most I could do was to make vague references to 'Hitler's last fling', and this made no impression on her.

In early August 1943 I heard that they were coming back. The children would arrive first as Iris would have to wind up her job while her successor was being found and trained, so I had to find and arrange schools for them and somewhere for us to live. An old friend let us have what had been her father's chauffeur's flat in Oxford Mews, Paddington. It was tiny and almost impossible to warm, as, owing to bombing, it had no heat from any other building, on either side or on top or bottom; but it was comfortable and we were together again, so what else mattered? It had a lot of sporting fun too; on most nights we could only enter by indulging in a sort of steeplechase over American soldiers in full blast on our doorstep with their girl-friends!

On the service side, I was as pressed as ever with the work that I have already described – broken only by a visit to Paris two weeks after its liberation. I had to go over to see Ginger Lewis who had become the Naval Intelligence Officer of S.H.A.E.F., Eisenhower's H.Q. It came at a busy time and could only just be fitted in.

In the train down to Newhaven there was an American Women's Army Corps Officer in our carriage and as she was very attractive I naturally carried her bag to the doorway through which the Americans went. As a result I found myself at the very end of a long, long queue of British officers waiting to have their travel papers checked at their exit. Newhaven was a naval port and a Chief Petty Officer stepped out of the office and shouted:

'Is Lieutenant-Commander Montagu there?'

'Yes, Chief,' I shouted back.

'Telephone message in the office for you, sir.' I walked past the queue cursing to myself – it could only be cancelling my journey and the whole time-table would be wrecked. So as I reached the door I asked,

'Do you know what it's about, Chief?' and he answered,

'Oh there's no message, sir, but I didn't see why you should wait behind all those bloody Pongos.' Trust the Navy to look after its own!

The liaison went well and I had some hours, up till midnight, free in Paris. I had taken over a number of pound packets of coffee for friends – both in the Services, and also a couple of civilians who lived there. It so happened that the last whom I tried to visit was away – so I had one packet left. I wondered what to do with it as I sat at a café having a drink on the pavement of the Champs-Elysées – it would obviously be a waste to take it home. Suddenly I had an inspiration as I saw an elderly *mère de famille*, in the usual black bombazine, dragging along four tired little children. I caught up, saluted and asked whether she would like some coffee. Having experienced the occupation she shrunk away – obviously fearing a trap. I explained what had happened in my broken French – and she seized the coffee, burst into tears and went off, clutching the elixir that she had missed for so long. It still remains one of the heart-warming memories of my life.

There was another event that occurred towards the end of the war, which brings an emotional memory to go with that of the old lady in Paris.

It started with a note from some department of the Admiralty : I was to go to Claridge's to get a medal from King Peter of Yugoslavia who was living there. We had worked a system through the double agents whereby we got several Yugoslav officers out of that country and to England. At our suggestion through a double agent, the Germans had 'recruited' them to 'spy' for Germany. After B.1A's case-officers had learnt their style, etc., they fought in the armed forces and we sent messages for them.

One of them was an ex-A.D.C. to King Peter. Without being aware of how we had rescued them from the Germans or of their 'notional spying', he was sufficiently grateful to give various classes of the Order of the Crown of Yugoslavia to 'C', the Director-General of M.I.5, J.C. Masterman, Tar Robertson, one of the case-officers and me. We assembled in the sitting-room of

King Peter's suite. He entered, explained charmingly that he could not give us the medals as they were not available in England yet, but he would give us the ribbons, and then read what seemed to be a hallowed formula starting: 'We, Peter, by the grace of God and the will of the people, King of Yugoslavia.' I wondered, did he know yet what I had seen scrawled on a newspaper poster outside the hotel, 'Tito chosen almost unanimously'? It seemed so tragic for him to have said 'by the will of the people' at that moment.

It did not matter that we never got the medals as the appropriate English authority thought that we had got them for 'personal services to the ruler', so we were only given 'conditional permission' to wear the decoration. As this virtually limits the permissible occasions to in the presence of the ruler (now Tito), at the embassy of the country involved, or in the country itself, to wear the Order of the Crown might be tantamount to attempted suicide!

The ribbon was dark blue with a little silver crown in the centre, and we were allowed to wear it during the war. The ribbon of the George Cross is dark blue with a little silver cross on it. The case-officer, who was a member of White's, was leaving that distinguished club when a Colonel Blimp-like member said, 'You're improperly dressed, young man. If you have the George Cross you should be proud of it. It comes first in the row, only behind the Victoria Cross, not right at the end where you've got it.' The young officer smiled at him and said, 'Oh, it's all right, sir – you see I won it posthumously,' and left while Colonel Blimp was trying to work that out.

As VE-day approached we were suddenly overwhelmed. Day after day we had to rush out 'special editions' of the Orange Summaries as more and more high-level messages reached us from Germany about collapse, the hopes of establishing a 'last redoubt' to carry on the war in Southern Germany, the advance of the Russian troops, damage by bombing, who was to take over from Hitler, intrigues, official decisions and so on – as well as Japanese messages about requests that they might intercede for peace. It was enthralling.

After the end of the war in Europe came a complete let down.

There was not a lot of active work for me to do. On the Special Intelligence side we still produced the Orange Summaries; the contents were mainly derived from the Japanese diplomatic traffic (usually to and from the Japanese ambassador in Moscow) which dealt with high political matters and even the possibility of *démarches* towards peace. On the deception side there was not much doing. We had lost our routes to the Japanese through the Germans but there seemed to be some prospect that new routes might be opened up in the East if the war continued for any length of time.

Captain Lambe, the Director of Plans, had informed me that there were two long-term deceptions that might usefully be pursued and we had been working on these before the surrender of Germany, in the hope of passing them to the Japanese through the Germans. Now he considered that these were worth completing in case the opportunity did arise to use them.

Both these schemes were concerned with designing and building warships of a novel kind. Both kinds would have been very useful indeed *if* they had been practicable. The schemes had, indeed, started as genuine design-operations and an immense amount of time and work had been put into them. Continually they 'very nearly worked' only for snags or complications to emerge which could not be overcome by the existing technology. Finally both schemes had been written off quite definitely and, as our boffins were satisfied that they were impracticable in the foreseeable future, Captain Lambe felt that it would be a good thing if we could divert Japanese technologists into as much unproductive effort and waste of time as ours had suffered.

The first of these schemes concerned what were referred to as 'battle-carriers'. These would have been ships which would have the armament and fighting ability of half a battle cruiser and which would also be able to carry and operate half the aircraft of a fleet aircraft carrier, as the Japanese navy had operated since 1943. This had apparently seemed to our pundits to be a very attractive proposition, but no amount of effort could produce anything which would not be inefficient in each role. It had been decided that the same effort and resources as would produce and man an efficient battle cruiser and an efficient aircraft carrier would be needed to produce and man two inefficient battle-carriers with the same total armament and aircraft.

The other scheme, which had been code-named Habbakuk, seemed so fantastic to me as a layman that at first I thought that Captain Lambe was pulling my leg. Could *anyone* be expected to believe that there was a genuine scheme to build aircraft carriers made out of ice? But it was genuine! Captain Lambe assured me that the scientists had, over a long period, kept on nearly solving the problems involved. It repeatedly 'nearly worked', but always yet another snag had appeared. So this scheme also had finally been written off, much to the disappointment of the Prime Minister for whom it had become a pet project. He probably cherished memories of the tanks that everyone else in the first war had said would not work.

Apparently the basic idea was to make the hulls on the Canadian, or at a later stage on the Alaskan, seaboard and install refrigeration machinery which would keep the hulls from melting. These hulls would carry the propulsive machinery, aircraft, crews and stores – as well as all the armament, ammunition and technical equipment. It seemed that, if the design could be got right, a vast amount of building time and shipbuilding manpower, and also of steel, would be saved, and all of these requisites were in desperately short supply for all the combatants.

Captain Lambe provided me with the documentation – the papers concerning the design, the snags and so on, and also the plans and drawings at various stages of the effort – as indeed he had done with the battle-carriers.

To my amazement, study of the Habbakuk plans did establish without doubt that the scheme would 'nearly work' – and, with technical help, I had got down to the further difficult job of producing a set of messages, documents and plans which would, as they were transmitted bit by bit to the Japanese, get them interested rather than completely sceptical, and then convinced enough to work on the two projects. The battle-carrier deception, in particular, could have the additional benefit that, if the Japanese were to believe that *we*, too, had in fact built efficient ships of this type, it could have an effect on their naval tactics and strategy beneficial to the Allies. So the work in preparing these two deceptions continued after VE-day.

However, Habbakuk was called off after a while. I understood that it was considered that, if by any chance Churchill got wind of this pet scheme of his being used for deception, it would have destroyed the relationship between him and the Admiralty whom he always had half suspected of not taking the project seriously enough.

On the other hand we got the battle-carrier deception scheme virtually ready for implementation, subject of course to the alterations which would have had to be made to any of the messages in order to make them suit the notional positions, jobs and characters of any double agents who could eventually be used to pass them across. Then came the atom bomb and the end of the war against Japan, so that this plan was never implemented.

One other point seems worth recording. We obviously had had to keep our eyes open to ensure that the Germans were not at any time working a double-cross on us – or even a treble-cross by realizing that one of our double-cross team was in fact double-crossing them and acting appropriately in order to deceive us and get real intelligence by properly interpreting the messages that we had intended as deception.

Here we had the inestimable advantage of reading Special Intelligence. The Abwehr wireless traffic made it quite clear that no treble-cross was happening at all. Their attempts at double-cross were very few indeed, and so futile and amateurish that their falsity could easily have been spotted even without the help of Special Intelligence.

The few instances that I can remember were in connection with one of 'C''s agents, Teapot, whom they had captured. They tried to put over through Teapot some misinformation about schnorkels, the apparatus through which U-boats got air while still submerged, and tried to suggest that these were having a lot of technical failures. They also tried to suggest that a particular area of the sea was dangerous by reporting that a ship, the *Leopoldville*, had been sunk by a mine. This report was so unconvincing in the way in which it had been put over to us that we would have seen through the stratagem even without the help given by the fact that, unfortunately for them, we had already read the U-boat's report of having sunk that ship with a torpedo!

I was able to include in my report that there was no doubt that the German efforts at deception through double agents were very few, very poor and amateurish, and wholly unsuccessful.

And so I carried on until the time came for me to go to the appropriate centre to get the civilian rig which was to be our parting present. When I got there the garments which were still available were all so awful that I chose the worst and loudest suit, ties and socks that I could find – they were wonderful for charades.

17

Tate's Triumph - The Phoney Minefield

When I look back at my war service, my memories usually seem to end with my last and most successful naval deception.

After the inter-Service deception to mislead the Germans about Overlord had proved such a success many who had been somewhat sceptical about the full potentialities of double agents changed their opinions. One of these was Captain Rodger Winn; he had been far too busy as Head of the U-boat Tracking Room in the O.I.C. to follow the successes that we had had; even Mincemeat was not a story that had come to his knowledge owing to the 'need to know' security principle. In consequence he had seemed to regard the deception side of my work as merely something that had appealed to Uncle John as a sort of harmless eccentricity. Our link over Special Intelligence had always been close, so he co-operated whenever I wanted something for deception purposes but there was no enthusiasm about it.

Now he clearly thought that I *might* be able to achieve something by this cloak-and-dagger charade, a description that he had once used, and he came up with a suggestion and a request.

Naval escort and anti-submarine vessels had been seriously over-stretched throughout the war, even with the assistance gained by the success of the anti-U-boat countermeasures carried on through the O.I.C., especially by the evasive routeing of convoys to avoid concentrations of U-boats. But the position got even more serious after D-day when many ships were needed for the protection of the steady flow of troops, armaments and supplies across the Channel.

One of the especial danger points for our shipping was the focal point where many sea-routes converged into the Western Approaches, something which had become even more serious when U-boats were fitted with schnorkels. When using this invention, snorting as we called it, U-boats no longer needed to surface to charge their batteries on which they ran submerged or to replenish the air needed for their crew to breathe. The schnorkel could be raised above water-level, while the U-boat itself remained invisible below the surface, and through it the poisonous diesel-exhaust fumes could be expelled and, simultaneously, fresh air could be drawn into the ship. The result was that they could remain below the surface for days at a time, completely hidden from air reconnaissance and merchant-ship look-outs – and even from warships until they got within Asdic range.

But there was one great difficulty that a U-boat would have to overcome when snorting at the end of its voyage from Germany or the Bay of Biscay – a difficulty which had faced seamen from time immemorial. As we know from all the celebrated wrecks round Cornwall, the Scilly Isles and the Atlantic coast of Ireland, a fix of the ship's position when making a landfall is vitally necessary. The U-boat Tracking Room had puzzled how the U-boats could fix their positions with the accuracy which was essential before approaching shallower waters and starting operations because, if they remained submerged in those comparatively heavily patrolled waters, they could get neither a normal celestial fix with a sextant nor even a radio-fix by taking bearings on transmissions from one of their shore stations. How did they do it? Now Rodger Winn was satisfied that he had found the answer.

Out to sea off the south coast of Ireland there is a point on the seabed which is unique and, equally important, could easily be found. Running submerged and with their depth sounders going the U-boats could pick up and follow identifiable contours on the sea-bed, if necessary for many miles from any direction, and continue to do so until they reached the point where the contour that they were following suddenly changed direction or depth. Perhaps it can best be explained by the analogy of, say, Mount Everest. If you follow one of the many ridges from any direction you will eventually reach the top where all ridges have finally converged; when you find that you can no longer follow your ridge you know that you are there – you know *exactly* where you are. And so did the U-boat captains.

Rodger Winn convinced the Director of Mining and the rest of the Naval Staff and all agreed that it was the ideal place to lay a minefield – not only with a likelihood of sinking some U-boats but, perhaps equally important, also of depriving them of this vitally important navigational aid. But the trouble was that there were no minelaying ships or mines that could be used. Both H.M.S. *Apollo* and H.M.S. *Plover*, the two ships which could have been used, were fully occupied, as far as I can remember, on the immediately essential task of laying all available mines in the Channel to protect our shipping supplying Normandy and there was therefore no possibility of carrying out the other operation, in spite of its importance.

So Rodger suggested to me that I might have a shot at scaring the U-boat captains off. As he put it, 'We won't sink any U-boats that way but the really important thing is to prevent their getting the fix that they need.' And then he smiled and added, 'And, anyway, you can't do any harm.'

Such a task seemed to be tailor-made for Tate. He had arrived by parachute in September 1940 and, as we knew that he was coming, he was duly collected by M.I.5. When interrogated he soon decided to co-operate in face of the knowledge, gained from Special Intelligence and other double agents, that he found we possessed about him. His early assignments from the Germans were largely concerned with the home front – production, food supplies and so on – but we, perhaps, built his credibility up mainly with the excellent naval information that he passed over.

It will be remembered that, early on, he had recruited Mary whom we had notionally placed in the American Naval H.Q. in Grosvenor Square. She had notionally been lent to the Americans when they first came over and were short of qualified staff, so that she could notionally see and learn high-level secrets.

Tate had got to know quite a number of naval officers, at first

directly through Mary who had known them in her Admiralty
days and then through one officer introducing another in 'social'
circumstances. This was the easier as Tate was very hospitable
with drinks and quiet parties. Having a great deal of money he
was well able to get drinks on the black market in spite of the
liquor shortage.

The only difficulty that arose, in spite of that background, over
the new deception about the non-existent minefield was that
Tate always communicated in terse telegraphese. How could
we convince the Germans that he not only knew that a secret
minefield had been laid but also where it was exactly? If he had
just reported that a new minefield had been laid so many miles
so many degrees South-West of the Fastnet Rock, or wherever
it was, any German would have asked how he could have learned
such detail.

But Tate's M.I.5 case-officer had become adept at conveying
the atmosphere behind a mere piece of information, in spite of
the telegraphese, and his German spy-master seemed capable of
reading between the lines. So this is the story that we put over.

One of the naval officers had become a particularly close
friend, often staying in the flat that Tate by now had in London;
he was a brash young man and, when they were sitting over a
series of night-caps in the flat, he was liable to get a little incautious in his conversation. He was a minelaying expert and
he made frequent visits to London, staying with Tate, to attend
conferences on new operations and to report on the completion
of others.

Now, on one evening, he let slip in a boastful moment: 'You
just wait and see, old man, we're going to get a good few U-
boats – we're laying a new minefield – I can't tell you where
but it's South of Ireland in a place where they go to fix their
position when they're snorting.' All of this Tate duly reported.

Next the officer stayed in the flat again on the completion of
the operation, and that was also reported to the Germans. For
a while there was no reaction by either the Abwehr or the German Navy that we could spot. And then we had a wonderful
stroke of luck which gave us the opportunity to clinch the matter.

A U-boat sank South of Ireland and the survivors were landed in Eire; this was made public, but no definite cause of the sinking was given though there was speculation about its having been caused by a mine – and no position was given. Further, we were confident from the U-boat traffic on Ultra that no signal had been got off before the U-boat sank. The actual position of the sinking was a long distance from our notional minefield and if the U-boat had hit a mine, it must have been a 'floater' which had drifted a long way from its original position since it broke away. But this gave us our opportunity.

Tate promptly radioed in an absolute fury. He was giving up, he said. What was the use of going on risking his life to get information if the Germans ignored it? The naval officer had come to stay the night after having had a celebration. He had been sent for by the Admiralty to be congratulated on the success of the minefield which had already sunk a U-boat, and he had been told that, for this on top of his other work, he might get a 'gong'. And Tate repeated that here was a U-boat and valuable lives thrown away through his report having been ignored. He was fed up.

The Germans replied with a soothing and reassuring message, which was nice for Tate and us, but something concrete followed.

A couple of days later Rodger Winn showed me an Ultra signal, one of the special operation orders to U-boats. This declared a prohibited area South of Ireland, forbidden to all U-boats; it was a square with sixty-mile sides – 3,600 square miles – so we had established a huge 'safe area' for our shipping in the Western Approaches. The prohibited area was centred on the underwater feature and covered the area that Tate's message had been intended to convey. Rodger Winn had, as so often, been right in his assessment, and the U-boat captains *had* been using that spot for their all-important fix, and they had now lost it forever.

That was the last of my frauds. As I've so often had old lags say to me since then, 'From now on I intend to go straight, M'Lord.'

Glossary

ABWEHR The German Military Intelligence Service under Admiral Canaris, reporting primarily to the German High Comand but, in effect, the secret service operating world-wide.

ABWEHR TRUPPEN Intelligence Commandos operating with the advanced troops to collect documents, material and other intelligence before they get dispersed.

A.C.N.S. Assistant Chief of the Naval Staff. There were two, A.C.N.S.(H) and A.C.N.S.(F), for home and foreign operations under the C.N.S. and V.C.N.S.(qv) in the Admiralty.

A.D.N.I. Assistant Director of Naval Intelligence, third ranking officer in the Naval Intelligence Division, traditionally a Royal Marine and in charge of security.

AST Intelligence headquarters established by the Abwehr in the capitals of occupied countries, as distinct from KOs (qv) in neutral capitals.

B.1A The Section of M.I.5 established to control and operate double agents.

B.P. Bletchley Park, the country house and ancillary buildings where intercepted enemy and neutral ciphered messages were deciphered and translated into English.

C. The initial by which the Head of the Secret Intelligence Service, M.I.6, was known. By transposition also normally used to refer to that Service itself.

CASE OFFICERS The officers of B.1A who controlled and operated a particular double agent or double agents.

CHICKEN FEED   Colloquial term for the information, not intended actually to deceive, which double agents were notionally (qv) allowed to pick up and which they were allowed to transmit to their German spy-masters (qv).

C.N.S.   Chief of the Naval Staff and First Sea Lord (1.S.L.)

D.D.N.I.   Deputy Director of Naval Intelligence, second in seniority to the Director.

D.M.I.   Director of Military Intelligence at the War Office.

D.N.I.   Director of Naval Intelligence at the Admiralty.

F.O.I.C.   Flag Officer in Command. The Admiral in command of an area, e.g. the Humber Command.

F.O.S.   Flag Officer Submarines. The Admiral in control of all submarines and submarine training, etc.

FUSAG   First United States Army Group. A non-existent force which we persuaded the Germans was preparing to invade France.

H.D.E.   Home Defence Executive. The civilian organization in charge of civilian defence, air raid precautions and similar activities in the United Kingdom.

1.S.L.   The First Sea Lord and Chief of the Naval Staff, also referred to as C.N.S.

I.S.S.B.   Inter Services Security Board. A committee of officers from each of the Services and a few others, in charge of the security of operations, particularly those to be mounted from the U.K.

J.I.C.   Joint Intelligence Committee composed of three Service Directors of Intelligence, C, the Director General of M.I.5, a representative of the Foreign Office (Chairman) and the Head of Special Operations Executive (see S.O.E.).

KO   Intelligence Headquarters established by the Abwehr in the capitals of neutral countries, as distinct from ASTs in occupied capitals.

KOSP   KO Spain in Madrid.

L.C.S.   London Controlling Section in charge of cover plans to deceive the Germans about our operations from 1942.

M.I.5   The Security Service responsible for security and counter-espionage in the United Kingdom and Commonwealth.

M.I.6   The Secret Intelligence Service responsible for collecting intelligence, our secret agents abroad and counter-espionage outside the Commonwealth. In spite of its title it was administered by the Foreign Office and was partially inter-Service. Also known as C after its Head.

M.P.I. Mean Point of Impact. The mean of the places of fall of the spread of bombs or other missiles during a raid or series of raids.

N.I.D. Naval Intelligence Division.

NOTIONAL Term used to denote something imaginary, other than the actual object of the deception, which the Germans were led to believe. For instance a notional job; or a double agent notionally went to Bristol and notionally saw a ship (which may or may not have been there).

O.I.C. The Operational Intelligence Centre in the Admiralty which co-ordinated all the intelligence relevant to actual operations and the movements of ships, etc., especially deciphered enemy signals, and advised the operational staff and commanders afloat. Numbered Section 8.

ORANGE SUMMARY The summary of non-operational deciphered signals with comments, provided to the First Lord, the First Sea Lord and the heads of the naval operational staff at least twice a day by Section 17M (qv).

S.D. The Sicherheitsdienst. The Nazi Party's intelligence and security service under Himmler. A rival of the Abwehr which, *inter alia*, controlled the GESTAPO.

SECTION 8s. Part of the O.I.C. (qv) which dealt with U-boats and controlled and manned the Submarine Tracking Room.

SECTION 17M The Section of N.I.D. of which the author was head and which is the subject of this book.

SECURITY CO-ORDINATION The organization in the United States, part of M.I.6, headed by Sir William (Little Bill) Stephenson, mainly to liaise with the F.B.I. and other U.S. intelligence agencies.

S.I.S. Secret Intelligence Service (see M.I.6).

S.O.E. Special Operations Executive established during the war to carry out sabotage, establish resistance groups, etc. in Germany and German occupied countries.

S.O.(I). Staff Officer (Intelligence). The naval intelligence officer on the staff of a Commander-in-Chief, Flag Officer or other naval commander.

SPY MASTER   The member of the Abwehr in Germany or an occupied or neutral country who actually controlled a spy or, from their point of view, controlled a double agent.

TRAFFIC   The messages sent by an agent or double agent to his spy-master, either chicken feed (qv) or actually to deceive.

TWENTY COMMITTEE   The inter-service committee which controlled the traffic that double agents transmitted. So called from the Latin numeral XX.

ULTRA   A name for Special Intelligence, deciphered messages and documents concerning them, denoted by the stamp TOP SECRET U. Derived from Ultra Secret.

V.C.N.S.   Vice Chief of the Naval Staff. The immediate subordinate of the First Sea Lord, C.N.S., particularly on all operational matters.

WAR REGISTRY   The department in the Admiralty which, *inter alia*, distributed all signals to those who should receive them.

W-BOARD   A committee of the three Service Directors of Intelligence and a few others which, for a period, met from time to time to supervise the Twenty Committee (qv).

XX   The symbol for double-cross. Hence the Twenty Committee (qv).

Index

F5